SACRED
WAITING

DAVID TIMMS

SACRED
WAITING

Waiting on God in a World That Waits for Nothing

BETHANY HOUSE
MINNEAPOLIS, MINNESOTA

Published by Bethany House Publishers
11400 Hampshire Avenue South
Bloomington, Minnesota 55438

Bethany House Publishers is a division of
Baker Publishing Group, Grand Rapids, Michigan.

Printed in the United States of America

In keeping with biblical principles of creation stewardship, Baker Publishing Group advocates the responsible use of our natural resources. As a member of the Green Press Initiative, our company uses recycled paper when possible. The text paper of this book is comprised of 30% post-consumer waste.

green
press
INITIATIVE

Library of Congress Cataloging-in-Publication Data

Timms, David.
    Sacred waiting : waiting on God in a world that waits for nothing / David Timms
        p.   cm.
    Summary: "Examines waiting on God as an aspect of spiritual formation, showing that we learn patience, obedience, and trust through waiting. Includes biblical examples of waiting as well as illustrations from the church calendar"—Provided by publisher.
    Includes bibliographical references.
    ISBN 978-0-7642-0678-8 (pbk. : alk. paper)   1. Spiritual life—Christianity.   2. Patience—Religious aspects—Christianity.   3. Trust in God—Christianity.
I. Title.
    BV4647.P3T56   2009
    248.4'6—dc22

                                                                2009025131

To my wife, Kim—
my beloved partner in "sacred waiting"

DAVID TIMMS

David Timms teaches New Testament and Theology and serves as chair of the Graduate Ministry Department at Hope International University in Fullerton, California. Australian by birth, David has been a church planter, pastor, and trainer of pastors for twenty-five years. He publishes an e-zine, *In Hope*, that shares his reflections on Christian leadership and spiritual formation. He and his wife, Kim, have three sons and live in Fullerton, California.

ACKNOWLEDGMENTS

Writing a book is much like building a house. It takes a team. On a building site, some folks dig trenches and pour foundations that will never be seen, others come along later and put in wall studs and wiring that will be hidden behind Sheetrock, and at the end a few folks do the painting that gives the project its final look. In many ways I'm just the painter.

This book reflects the wisdom, insights, and input of many people—more than I can mention, but whose investment in my life or whose passing comments have helped build the house. That team includes people from the past who invested in digging the foundations (mentoring and nurturing me)—people like John and Kae Thornhill, John and Helen York, and my parents, John and Pam Timms.

The team also includes more recent tradespeople assembled by the Master Builder. Kyle Duncan at Bethany House has shown great faith in this project, while Ellen Chalifoux, my editor, did much of the cutting and finishing work. My dear friends Scott and Stephanie Rosner devoted many hours to reading a draft manuscript and offering much needed guidance, and the administration at Hope International University encouraged me to keep writing. My sincerest and deepest thanks to each of you.

I also want to acknowledge the online *In Hope* community—hundreds of fellow workers for the Kingdom who graciously receive my regular email reflections. Your feedback (and occasional push-back) has shaped me—and this book—in many subtle ways.

A special thanks also to my three sons—Matthew, Caleb, and Joel. You guys inspire me and keep my feet on the ground at the same time. And to Kim, who for two and a half decades of marriage has patiently and lovingly invested in me. You amaze me with your love, your attentiveness, and your faith.

None of this happens, of course, without the Architect and Master Builder, our Father. All honor to the Father, the Son, and the Holy Spirit, to whom belong the Kingdom, the power, and the glory forever.

CONTENTS

Introduction   11

    1. Noah: Wait and Endure   22

    2. Abraham: Wait and Trust   36

    3. Moses: Wait and Learn   51

    4. David: Wait and Worship   65

    5. Jesus: Wait and Obey   80

Transition   96

    6. The Advent Wait   98

    7. The Lenten Wait   111

    8. The Easter Wait   124

    9. The Pentecost Wait   138

    10. The Kingdom Wait   153

Postscript   167

Endnotes   173

INTRODUCTION

Eternal God, who heals my hurts and restores my soul, teach me to wait on you not for what I might receive but for what I might give. Still my hurried heart to hear you this day. Amen.

We live in a world that waits for nothing. Abstinence programs have limited appeal. Young couples regularly overextend themselves. Families live beyond their means. We have, for the most part, shaken off restraint and embraced a stunning degree of materialism, consumerism, and hedonism. Comfort and pleasure have become the supreme goals of life. And we pursue it with credit and debt.

In 2006, Americans held about 984 million Visa and Master-card accounts—three for every man, woman, and child in the country—and by the end of 2008, the total consumer debt in the United States had reached $2.56 *trillion*.[1] If we take that staggering figure and spread it across the total population, it means that personal household debt at that time amounted to about $8,400 for every individual. And that excludes any home mortgage debt.

Clever advertising fuels the credit craze by insisting that we need not wait for what we want. In fact, we can have it now and pay for it later—much later, in some instances.

In past generations, when credit was not so readily available, eating out, getting gasoline, buying clothes, making small home improvements, and a dozen other regular expenses were all paid for with cash, or folks waited. Our culture has long since wearied of waiting.

The pace of life that we embrace means that every wait represents a waste of our time. So we grumble when the computer takes two minutes to boot up. We eat a lot of fast food. We live attached to our cell phones or BlackBerrys so we can quickly pick up every call, text message, or email—even while on vacation. We view the yellow traffic light as an invitation to "put the pedal to the metal" rather than brake. Then we grow impatient if the traffic lights remain red for long. Our irritation level rises exponentially in checkout lines, train stations, restaurants, and doctors' offices—not to mention the dreaded Department of Motor Vehicles. None of us likes to wait. There's simply too much to do!

THE PACE OF LIFE

Until the eighteenth century, the pace of life rarely exceeded the walking pace of a horse. People traveled short distances at relatively slow speeds. Or if they went far, they took a long time to do so. Twenty miles was considered a solid day's ride. But with the Industrial Revolution all of that changed. Steam-powered ships, railways, and mass-produced motor vehicles began to accelerate the pace.

In more recent times, that pace has increased even further. In the 1970s, we communicated with letters that we could send quickly—even overnight—by various mail carriers. In the 1980s, we enjoyed faster communication through fax machines. In the 1990s, the rise of email let us send out more messages than ever before, as long as we had access to a computer. In the 2000s, we've turned to text messaging with its own shorthand—LOL, BFF, CU—that communicates in ultra-short messages rather than expressive pages. Facebook and Twitter keep our friends and subscribers constantly aware of what's happening with us. Communication, which should involve deeper knowledge of each other, has diminished to quick and usually superficial levels.

Recently one of my sons managed to exchange 3,000 text messages in one of his first months with a cell phone. When I mentioned this to some friends, they shared that their daughter had racked up 13,000 text messages in the same period—433 text messages every day of the month; an average of one message about every two minutes of every waking hour for a month. Quick, brief, and constant communication has dramatically changed the number of demands we have to juggle in any given day.

As the speed of our lives increases, the quality of our relationships usually decreases.

An interesting study carried out in the early 1990s demonstrated that the speed at which pedestrians walk provides a reliable measure of the pace of life in a city, and that people in fast-moving cities are less likely to help others, and have higher rates of coronary heart disease. Research teams discovered that the pace of life rose 10 percent over a decade in many cities. The researchers simply measured the time it took for people, unaware that they were being studied, to walk sixty feet. Interestingly, Singapore emerged as the fastest city in the world by this measurement, with the average pedestrian covering sixty feet in a zippy 10.55 seconds.[2]

All of this highlights the exponential increase in our pace of life, something we hardly need to be told. And the impact on our relationships and quality of life is proving devastating. A fundamental principle holds true: *As the speed of our lives increases, the quality of our relationships usually decreases.*

We've all had this experience. The workplace adds increasing pressure, stress, and time demands that result, inevitably, in less time with a spouse and children, less time in meaningful relational groups, and less time with friends. The increased speed at work has a corollary—poorer relationships everywhere else. Similarly, when we sit at lunch watching the clock, it's hard to fully engage with the person across the table. Faster lives diminish our meaningful connections.

Of course, some occasions demand speed. When the building catches fire, we had better race out rather than chat on a sofa with someone. But our time-oriented culture has put such a squeeze on every waking moment that it's little wonder marriages continue to collapse at an alarming rate, and we simply dream about meaningful friendships rather than experience them.

We live in a world that waits for nothing—and it's killing us in more ways than we know.

HURRYING (PAST) GOD

In the midst of our mad scramble—what we bravely but vainly call the "good life"—we also find ourselves harboring deep-seated impatience with God. We have little time to nurture a relationship with Him and generally feel that He should run at least as fast as we do. If we have a problem right now, then right now would be a good time for the Lord to step in and deal with it. We squeeze in a quick prayer request while changing lanes in rush-hour traffic and expect the Lord to fire back a quick answer, preferably a positive one. All the while we're rushing Him and rushing past Him.

On January 12, 2007, world-renowned violinist Joshua Bell participated in an experiment organized by the *Washington Post.*

Three days earlier Bell had played at Boston's stately Symphony Hall, where concert patrons had paid at least $100 per ticket to hear the virtuoso. For the experiment, he agreed to be a busker at a Washington, D.C. metro train station where people could lean against a wall and listen to him for free.

Wearing a long-sleeved T-shirt and a Washington Nationals baseball cap, Bell treated the commuter crowd to some of the greatest violin music ever composed. For forty-three minutes at L'Enfant Plaza, as low-level bureaucrats got off their trains on the way to work, he delivered masterpieces by Bach, Schubert, and others. Not only did he play some of the most moving pieces ever written, but he did so on his $3.5 million violin—a 300-year-old Stradivarius.

> Three minutes went by before *something* happened. Sixty-three people had already passed when, finally, there was a breakthrough of sorts. A middle-aged man altered his gait for a split second, turning his head to notice that there seemed to be some guy playing music. Yes, the man kept walking, but it was something.
>
> A half-minute later, Bell got his first donation. A woman threw in a buck and scooted off. It was not until six minutes into the performance that someone actually stood against a wall, and listened.
>
> Things never got much better. In the three-quarters of an hour that Joshua Bell played, seven people stopped what they were doing to hang around and take in the performance, at least for a minute. Twenty-seven gave money, most of them on the run—for a total of $32 and change. That leaves the 1,070 people who hurried by, oblivious, many only three feet away, few even turning to look.[3]

How often do we do the same thing to God? We're in a hurry and expect God to address our concerns when we schedule time for Him. But life is generally far too pressing to "lean against a wall and listen." Many of us would excuse the poor train commuters. After all, they had places to be. Why would they stop when they were watching the clock? Who wants to be late for work? And that's precisely the point. Their hurry deafened them to the extraordinary music reverberating around the metro that morning. In the same way, our hurry through life threatens to blunt our awareness of the extraordinary Presence of Christ who sits so much more quietly in the wings of our lives. Aren't most of us watching the clock most of the time?

THE BIBLE AND WAITING

Throughout the Scriptures we read the stories of men and women who learned the significance of waiting and the peril of rushing. The prophet Isaiah declared to the people of his day, "They that wait upon the LORD shall renew their strength" (Isaiah 40:31 KJV). Several centuries earlier, the psalmist sang with the confidence of someone who has discovered an important secret: "My soul waits in silence for God only" (Psalm 62:1 NASB). Jesus, after His resurrection, did not drive His disciples out into the world in a frenzied bid to do as much as possible as fast as possible. Instead, He instructed them to wait in Jerusalem (see Acts 1:4).

In Scripture, waiting is not an option but a mandate.

Wait. Wait. Wait. We don't have time to waste. Life feels too short, the opportunities (and needs) too many. Besides, he who hesitates is lost. But time and again, God calls us to wait. He refuses to fit our demands and schedules. In contrast, He expects us to conform to His plans and rely on His timing. And in the process we learn deep, transforming truths.

Waiting on God runs against every cultural instinct that we

have. We wait for nothing. Yet we find that in Scripture, waiting is not an option but a mandate.

DEFINING THE TERMS

When our family eats out, we usually hit fast-food chains—with coupons. But occasionally we splurge and sit down in a restaurant. The chief difference, apart from the price, is that these nicer establishments have *waiters,* and these table waiters can teach us much about the biblical concept of waiting.

Typically, when we think of waiting, we think of killing time until our goal or destination is reached. Waiting for the bus to arrive means standing idly until it finally pulls up at the curb. Waiting for graduation means counting down the days until we receive our diploma. Waiting for medical attention means hanging on until we can be treated. In other words, waiting represents what we have to do between two points in time to get what we really want.

Sacred waiting—waiting on God—is nothing like that.

The restaurant waiter has two main tasks. First, greeting us (which may include chatting with us, listening to us, and just being present with us). The initial responsibility is to make us feel welcome, comfortable, and at ease. Waiting on us means being present with us and building a connection with us, albeit briefly, because a waiter is usually waiting on others, too. But we shouldn't overlook this element of "presence."

Second, the waiter serves us. (Actually, waiters are more often called servers today.) He waits on us by attending to our specific requests when we make them, meeting our needs when he sees them, and serving our food. His service is fundamental. A happy waiter who fails to deliver what we ask for has failed his responsibility.

Biblically speaking, this forms the essence of waiting on God: *presence* and *service,* which involve drawing closer to Him and responding to His leading. It's vastly different from the way in which we typically use the word *wait*. We're not watching the clock. We're not counting down to some particular event or calling. Rather, a lifetime of waiting on God reflects a lifetime of simple presence and service.

Along the way, a great many things happen. The Father makes requests that may take a lot of time. He makes promises without delineating time frames. He remains relatively silent for long periods. We suffer distractions and hardships. Nevertheless, the deeper spiritual journey—sacred waiting—leads us to the classic vocation of the table waiter: his presence with us and his service to us.

In the chapters to follow, these two criteria will dominate our definition of waiting. We'll learn to steer away from the toe-tapping impatience that waiting usually evokes from us, and we'll learn to embrace presence and service in a fresh way. Such an embrace will take us a long way toward minimizing the impatience and frustration we may feel in our faith and maximizing the joy and peace of His table.

GETTING IT STRAIGHT

Unfortunately, when it comes to spiritual realities, we often turn them completely around. We act as though God must wait upon us. We carve out a few minutes for Him here and there and expect Him to jump to attention when we call on Him. He is always waiting for us to come to Him, people tell us. He is the endlessly patient Father. Perhaps the story that Jesus told of the extravagantly wasteful (prodigal) son, in Luke 15, reinforces this view that when we finally hit rock bottom and come to our senses we can be sure that the Father is waiting for us to return. That's His role, it seems, while ours is to scurry around in life and keep checking in with Him from time to time—like the table waiter with multiple tables to serve. Each time He will gratefully receive what little attention we might give Him. But such thinking violates a fundamental biblical truth: The task of waiting falls far more to *us* than to Him.

Our prayer lives often betray this false thinking, too. How many of us use prayer as a time to tell the Father what *we* need and what *we* think would be best?

> *The task of waiting falls far more to* us *than to Him.*

"Lord, if you didn't already know it, let me tell you that this knee is really bothering me. Would you give me some pain relief today?"

"Lord, that family over there could sure use your attention right now. They've just lost a grandmother, and it would be nice if you could serve up a special dose of peace and comfort to them."

"Father, I've got a big day ahead at work, could you give me an extra helping of wisdom?"

"Well, Lord, it's the end of the day. Thanks for being with me. Now, if you'd stay on duty throughout the night, too, and watch over me, that would be great. Thanks."

Such prayers sound suspiciously like menu orders at a restaurant: *we're placing the orders rather than receiving them.* Of course, the Bible encourages us to make petitions and requests of God. The apostle Paul did not hesitate to write: "Present your requests to God" (Philippians 4:6). And the Lord cares deeply for us and the issues of life that touch us. However, we too easily cross the line and begin to view Him as our servant rather than ourselves as His slaves. And our prayers become a barometer of our attitude. We can't seem to get it straight. We use prayer to get His attention rather than quietly giving Him ours.

The Bible suggests that the onus for waiting lies with us. The heroes of the faith all waited on Him. Their best moments arose from God's timing, not their own. Indeed, God establishes all the glorious covenants of Scripture after significant seasons of sacred waiting on the part of His servants.

Noah walked with God—waited on Him—for 600 years before the rainbow covenant was established after the flood (see Genesis 6–9). Abraham listened to the Lord and obeyed Him for nearly 100 years before the son of the promise would be born (see Genesis 12:1–4; 21:5). Moses was ready to do his bit to support his fellow Israelites when he killed a harsh Egyptian taskmaster (see Exodus 2:11–12), but he had to wait on the Lord for forty years in the desert before the Lord sent him back to Egypt to deliver the people (see Exodus 3:10). David had been chosen and anointed to succeed Saul as king of Israel, but he waited on God for over a decade before he eventually took the mantle.

Henri Nouwen, one of the great spiritual writers of the late twentieth century, wrote: "For many people, waiting is an awful desert between where they are and where they want to go."[4] He's right. But sacred waiting teaches us to embrace the desert and relinquish our own plans.

DIFFERENT JOURNEYS

While the elements of sacred waiting remain the same—presence and service—the outcomes vary enormously. As we'll see throughout this book, waiting on God produced different experiences for each person and shaped each one differently. Each person learned unique life-altering lessons as they waited on God. Their presence and service to the Lord did not yield the same outcome in every case.

Noah learned endurance. Abraham grew in his trust of God. Moses emptied himself. David discovered new depths of worship. And Jesus learned obedience.

As we practice the art and discipline of sacred waiting, we'll discover that its outcomes differ for each of us, too. But we will see a common thread: attentiveness (presence) and obedience (service) to Christ. Sometimes we'll find ourselves very still; other times very active. Occasionally waiting on the Lord will require solitude on our part so that all the surrounding sounds can be eliminated and we can hear Him more clearly. Other times waiting on Him will be an exercise in serving others "as unto Christ." One thing is certain: We will only wait on Him with joy if we have deep confidence in His love for us.

May the chapters ahead encourage and equip you for sacred waiting, and for the joy, peace, and abundance that it always yields.

GROUP DISCUSSION

1. Describe some of the symptoms of "hurry-up" in your own life. Does this feel under control or out of control?

2. Consider the analogy of the table waiter. Is this helpful to you in thinking about waiting on God? What else comes to mind as you consider this analogy?

3. This chapter defines sacred waiting in terms of our presence and service to the Father. How do these two terms complement each other?

4. How can we get it straight in terms of who waits on whom? What are some small steps you might take to increasingly give God the seat of honor in your life?

5. Discuss some ways in which you might be more attentive to Him (wait on Him).

CHAPTER 1

NOAH: WAIT AND ENDURE

God of the ages, vast and past, slow me down to walk with you; not rushing to achieve my own projects this day, but content in yours. Grant me the courage to wait on you when ridicule or confusion comes, and the endurance to persist when the end is not clear. Amen.

On February 26, 2008, Starbucks took an unprecedented step. It shut its doors across America—for three hours. More than seven thousand Starbucks stores throughout the U.S. closed at 5:30 PM, local time, "for a teach-in that was part espresso tutorial, part pep rally."[1] One hundred thirty-five thousand baristas received the training.

Why such a drastic measure? Starbucks' stock value had fallen about 50 percent in the preceding twelve months. Company management attributed part of that slide to increasingly poor service and flagging morale. Thus they organized an innovative, national, publicly advertised training session. The unprecedented step was designed to send a strong message to Starbucks customers: "The company is committed to better service." So when Chief Executive Howard Schultz sent out the memo, all stores had to comply.

In Genesis 6, Noah received his own newsworthy "memo"—to build an ark. However, unlike Starbucks' baristas, the mandate took Noah into areas of service that he had never before considered. The request probably meant closing down his family business—whatever that was—and took considerably more than an evening to fulfill. It made little sense, and it drew Noah away from a comfortable lifestyle he probably enjoyed.

The story of Noah contains important elements that we often overlook when we consider waiting on the Lord. Noah waited on God—presence and service—in an extraordinary way and for an extraordinary length of time. His story reveals profound truths to guide us as we engage in sacred waiting.

A STRONG HERITAGE

When Noah was born, both his father, Lamech, and grandfather, Methuselah, were alive and well. His dad had lived 182 years already—a little old to start a family by our standards, but not unusual in those days. Grandpa had just celebrated his birthday and seemed strong. He was 369! It turns out that for that era he had not even reached middle age. Everyone in the family told stories about Great-Grandpa Enoch, who had died before Noah's birth. People said that he walked with God and knew God so well that eventually God just took him (see Genesis 5:22, 24). As the story passed down through the kids and grandkids, it inspired many of them—especially Noah. He wanted to walk with God, too.

Grandpa Methuselah, who never seemed to age, had a name that intrigued everyone. It meant something like "when he dies, it will be sent."[2] Huh? What will be sent? This curiosity was periodically discussed around family dinners.

And Noah's own name sounded odd: "Rest." His father, Lamech, had said at Noah's birth, "This one will give us *rest* from our work and from the toil of our hands arising from the ground which the LORD has cursed" (Genesis 5:29 NASB). How would Noah accomplish that? It all seemed rather strange. So between grandfather and grandson, the family speculated a lot about the future—watching grandpa's health and Noah's actions.

FIVE CENTURIES OF FAITHFULNESS

Oddly enough, considering that God preserved only Noah and his immediate family through the catastrophic flood, we don't know much about the first 480 years of Noah's life, except that during that period he apparently took the stories about Great-Grandpa Enoch to heart. He learned to walk with God. The writer of Genesis puts it very succinctly: "Noah found favor in the eyes of the LORD. . . . Noah was a righteous man, blameless among the people of his time, and he walked with God" (Genesis 6:8–9).

We have no indication in the Bible that God used Noah mightily throughout those first five *centuries* of his life; no suggestion that Noah's godliness changed the world or that his faith touched the lives of anyone. In fact, just the opposite was true. During that time, the world around him descended into such utter chaos and corruption that God purposed to destroy it. But when God called Noah to build an ark—to prepare for the most destructive event in world history—Noah had no doubt who was speaking.

I spend a lot of time with people who want to clarify the call of God on their lives. For example, Dan, a thirty-something salesman, wants to sort out whether or not God has called him to church ministry. He's impatient because he feels the years slipping away so quickly. Then there's Bill, approaching retirement, who wants a clear word from the Lord about his own next season of life. Should it be teaching, pastoring, or business-building for the Kingdom? In a world filled with pain, heartache, violence, and corruption, many of us want to make a difference, a significant difference. So we agonize over what we should *do* rather than learning to walk with God. Perhaps we rationalize that we'll have eternity to walk with God, but that right now there's work to be done. Noah's life story reminds us to wait on the Lord—presence and service, in that order.

Of course, when the Father "places His order," it may have little to do with our abilities, training, or personal vision for the future. I'd be surprised to find that Noah was a boat builder by trade who had always anticipated the end of the world and had drafted plans for a giant zoo-ship. Yet we constantly assess God's leading by reviewing our passions, strengths, past experiences, and confirmation from others.

Noah's most strategically important qualification was not common sense but connection with the Lord. Walking with the Lord and waiting on the Lord are one and the same. For centuries Noah's heart grew softer as his spiritual sensitivity grew sharper. He had learned to be a table waiter to the Lord. Amidst the clamor and corruption around him, he remained supple and attuned to God, being fully present to Him and serving Him when directed. He models sacred waiting for us.

Noah demonstrates the importance of time spent learning to discern the voice of God. Those 480 years of walking with God made for a very definitive moment in the course of Noah's life and human history.

Noah's strategically important qualification was not common sense but connection with the Lord.

YOU WANT A WHAT?

For centuries God remained patient—patient with a people who defined cruelty and oppression and who moved further and further from His intentions, who took increasing delight in perversion and degradation. Finally He stepped in. As He observed the violence, the immorality, and the evil, "the LORD was sorry that He had made man on the earth, and He was grieved in His heart" (Genesis 6:6 NASB). He gave a word—a clear and unmistakable word—to Noah:

"Build an ark."

"I beg your pardon?"

"Build an enormous, floating shoe box for you, your family, and all the animals I send you."

"How big will that have to be?"

"About half the size of the *Titanic*—roughly 450 feet long, 75 feet wide, and 45 feet high, with about 100,000 square feet of deck space."[3]

"Oh. That's about what I would have figured!"

What a task. Noah couldn't just run down to the local lumber yard and order the timber he needed. The ark would take nearly 18,000 planks (eight feet long by four inches wide) *just to make the outer shell*! Add to that all the gopher wood for the beams, floors, and ribs, and the amount of timber that must be hand-hewn becomes staggering. Simply gathering the timber presented an enormous logistical challenge. And without four-inch galvanized nails, power tools, or mechanical cranes, the construction demanded great patience and enormous endurance.

We can only begin to imagine the ecological changes Noah produced while building the ark. How many gopher trees did he fell on his own land and the land of his neighbors? The ark required thousands of them.[4]

Genesis 6:3 indicates that this project probably spanned 120 years, which under the circumstances just described, may have felt like a rush order. We know for sure that Noah was 600 years old when the flood came (Genesis 7:6). His father, Lamech, had died five years earlier, and Grandpa Methuselah died in the year that God sent the flood, fulfilling the prophetic meaning of his name: "When he dies, it will be sent." Then the fountains of the deep burst open and the rains started—torrential, soaking, flooding, pounding, drowning rains.

Noah had worked twelve decades for this moment, though he surely never imagined how swift and devastating the flood would actually be. And then, as if 120 years of preparation were not enough, he and his family had to stay on board that floating menagerie for more than a year before the waters subsided enough for them to leave it.[5] The word *wait* never appears in the biblical narrative, but the story is baptized in it.

WAITING WITH ENDURANCE

If we assume that waiting on God means putting our feet up and sipping soft drinks until He touches base with us, we misunderstand it entirely. Sacred waiting has always involved both presence and service.

As we consider Noah's story in the book of Genesis, we see a lapse of years between the following verses.

> Noah did everything just as God commanded him.
>
> Genesis 6:22

> The LORD then said to Noah, "Go into the ark. . . ."
>
> Genesis 7:1

Between these two consecutive verses in Scripture lie 120 years—a lifetime and a half for us—of hard labor, of ridicule from friends, family, and neighbors, of blisters, calluses, splinters, and injuries. Yet those 120 years surely incorporated both presence and service, and we can assume that Noah continued to walk with God as he worked diligently to fulfill the commission of the Lord. Decade after decade Noah persisted with the task, learning exceptional endurance, even though he could not have imagined how it would all eventually play out.

None of us would find such a physical undertaking easy, especially once we turned 500! But Noah's incredible diligence and forbearance stand as a challenge to us. Sacred waiting never questions the timing or the size of the Father's request. For 480 years, Noah watched the increasing decadence of society around him, powerless to change the godlessness, and surely grieved by the sin. Yet throughout those years he gently attended the table of the Lord with his presence and service. Then came the commissioning of the ark. God's patience had ended, and Noah's hard labor had just begun—and would last a very long time.

When the construction was complete, the Lord delivered the dramatic order: "Enter the ark, you and all your household . . ." (Genesis 7:1 NASB).

HIS TIMING

The notion that waiting always corresponds with stillness, inactivity, or idleness certainly was not an interpretation passed down to us from Noah. Just when we decide that waiting on the Lord means quitting everything and sitting cross-legged under a tall and shady tree, Noah throws a curve ball.

Sacred waiting had at least three facets for Noah: getting to know the Lord intimately (presence), responding obediently (service), and trusting His timing in all things.

Two of my sons have played baseball. In Joel's AA season, the players, mostly age eight or nine, learned the art of stealing bases for the first time. T-ballers, rookies, and single-A players don't get to steal, since it can take two cut-off throws just to get the ball from home plate to second base. But AA players start to mimic the major leaguers.

As Coach Mike and Coach Rod trained the boys in the fine art of base stealing, it seemed to me that the training shared the three facets of waiting on God: (1) recognize the voice of your coach; (2) run immediately when the coach says "Go!"; and (3) trust that the coach's sense of timing is better than your own. The coach, after all, is watching the entire field and can see the whole play unfolding. The runner must remain focused entirely on the next base.

Getting ready to steal involves skipping out a couple of steps from the base and being poised to spring into action. A successful stolen base requires attentiveness, cooperation, and partnership. But no one calls it easy or relaxed! As the boys learned this skill, some would slide and end up short of the base; others would bounce along the ground; a few would flip, roll, and tumble.

The worst base running happens, however, when a dad behind the dugout yells at his son to run. The boy must differentiate between the voices of the crowd—some of which sound very familiar—and the voice of the coach. And success only comes through compliance with the one voice of authority; in this case, the coach.

Noah's story challenges us to live life walking with God so that we can best serve Him, even if He calls us to a long and difficult task. It evokes both senses of the word *wait*—that we learn to practice His Presence and always stand ready to serve when He speaks. But Noah's experience also teaches us to trust the Lord's timing, which might require deep reserves of endurance from us.

Of course, many of us do not hesitate to roll up our sleeves and help people. We're comfortable with the call to action. Besides, our culture honors activists, and *busy* remains a compliment. We'll join a committee, serve in a church ministry, give generously to the food pantry, and perhaps even make a short-term mission trip to serve Christ—all of which is generous, but it may not be an example of waiting on Christ. If we're not attentive, we can easily fill our lives with tasks of little consequence and no connection with the leading of the Lord. Service always *follows* presence. First we learn to walk with God; meaningful service springs from that relationship.

> *If we're not attentive, we can easily fill our lives with tasks of little consequence.*

Noah took 480 years learning the voice of God before he received his monumental commission. How might our lives change if we moved more in God's timing than in our own planning? It may not take the better part of five centuries for us to detect and define God's voice (let's hope not!), but will we listen for Him or plow ahead on our own? Attentiveness to Him, which usually begins on our knees in prayer, followed promptly by our obedience, invariably achieves His purposes.

Barbara Brown Taylor, an outstanding Bible teacher and preacher, tells the story of a friend who traveled to visit her shortly after she moved from Atlanta to the small township of Clarkesville in the north Georgia foothills. Without a cell phone or a reliable map, the friend became hopelessly lost, increasingly frantic, and somewhat faster on the roads. Finally, she glanced in her rearview mirror and saw those ominous flashing blue lights. She pulled over, and as the police officer approached her driver's side window, she handed him her license and registration. "I am so sorry," she said. "I know I was speeding, but I've been lost for the last forty minutes, and I cannot find Tower Terrace anywhere on this map." "Well, I'm sorry about that, too, ma'am," he said, writing up her citation, "but what made you think that hurrying would help you find your way?"[6]

TRUE TO THE DREAM OR THE DREAM GIVER

At the 2007 National Youth Worker's Convention in San Diego, Phil Vischer, creator of *VeggieTales*, told the story about the rise and fall of his Big Idea Productions and the many lessons he learned through the process. He had founded the company, in July 1993, to produce a series of videos based on animated cartoon figures. But through a long series of poor business decisions and difficulties with their facilities, the business faltered and had to be sold, despite the enormous popularity of *VeggieTales*.

As Vischer addressed conferees, he challenged them with the question, "What is more important to you: the dream or God?" He highlighted that God gives us dreams, but sometimes we let those dreams take control of us and we stop seeking God's heart. We need to learn how to wait on God—a critically important step to prevent the dream itself from becoming an idol. Indeed, our greatest impact only happens when we seek God, not impact. In essence, Phil Vischer was describing Noah's experience.

Noah could easily have grown consumed with the ark project. While he did not have to organize a capital campaign to go along with it—that we know of—the work surely demanded most of his mental and physical energy. How easy it would be, after ten or twenty years, for Noah to lose sight of God and see only the task before him. Perhaps you've been in shorter church building programs and experienced the same temptation. But the ark project never became Noah's. It always remained God's. Indeed, decades later Noah seemed to walk as closely with the Lord as ever.

Noah learned to discern the voice of God and listen to it. When the word came—"Build an ark"—the Bible does not indicate any argument from Noah, or delay. He got straight to it. And Noah obeyed right down to the particulars. The Lord specified gopher wood for the construction, so Noah used gopher wood. He did not substitute the great cedars of Lebanon or the oaks of Mamre. And Noah stuck to the task to the end, despite the assignment taking 120 years. Year after year he served consistently and persistently, with nary a growl or a grumble. And the Lord achieved His purposes.

Noah's example includes remarkable faithfulness to the Lord. After fifty years at the task without a raindrop in sight, after a hundred years of backbreaking toil, many of us would likely have wondered if this was a worthy demand. But Noah remained steadfastly confident that God, who sees from beginning to end, had the perfect timing.

How might you assess your own status as God's *waiter* when the years seem to roll by with tiring toil? Would you persist with a task that might mean a lifetime without glory or fame? Or do you find yourself energetic and enthusiastic for the short-term but disinterested for the long haul?

Noah waited on the Lord remarkably. Will we do the same?

WAITING AND THE COVENANT

After the flood, God honored Noah. We shouldn't think of it as a tip for good service, but we will see a pattern as we examine Old Testament lives in the first half of this book. Following Noah's presence and service, God established a covenant with him that would be a blessing to all of us.

Once the earth had dried sufficiently for Noah and his family and all the animals to leave the ark, we read:

> Then Noah built an altar to the LORD and, taking some of all the clean animals and clean birds, he sacrificed burnt offerings on it. The LORD smelled the pleasing aroma and said in his heart:

"Never again will I curse the ground because of man. . . . Never again will I destroy all living creatures, as I have done. . . . I establish my covenant with you: Never again will all life be cut off by the waters of a flood; never again will there be a flood to destroy the earth." And God said, "This is the sign of the covenant I am making between me and you and every living creature with you, a covenant for all generations to come: I have set my rainbow in the clouds, and it will be the sign of the covenant between me and the earth."

Genesis 8:20–21; 9:11–13

This covenant agreement, that God would never again destroy the world with a flood, surely came as good news to Noah. We ought not underestimate the horrors of that deluge; people pounding on the sides of the ark as the waters rose, desperately seeking a way on board; the bloated bodies of animals and people floating for weeks, if not months; the devastation of everything Noah had known his entire life, and the displacement to a strange place after being adrift for so long. The ark was no cruise liner, and this voyage did not return cheery vacationers to their cozy homes. Yes, this covenant came as profoundly good news after the frightening unleashing of God's judgment.

However, the covenant extended well beyond Noah's small circle. His faithfulness produced a blessing for all humanity ever since. Regional floods still happen. Natural catastrophes still occur. But never again will God destroy the entire world by flood.

NOAH AND US

None of us can consider Noah's remarkable story without affirming that God honors those who wait upon Him. Indeed, Noah's experience of waiting on God serves as an important model for us.

Noah exercised extraordinary perseverance to wait on God as

he did. The same might be required of us. And that kind of staying power flows not from a strong will but from a walk with the Lord. Too often we view endurance as the by-product of teeth-gritting determination. We tend to have low forbearance levels for proclaiming the Kingdom message or doing Kingdom tasks that attract criticism or opposition. We'll serve Christ as long as we see some immediate results. Discouragement sets in quickly if we can't see progress—even when we believe that Christ has called us to a particular service.

Noah's story calls us to reestablish the dimensions of waiting that make endurance truly possible—presence, then service. We walk with God so we can serve Him well. Our walk with the Lord begins and sustains the process.

> *If you're struggling, perhaps it's because the work flows not from your walk but from your will.*

Perhaps you've struggled to endure through tough times as a follower of Jesus. Many of us have. Such struggles often arise because we fail to nurture the presence side of waiting and practice only the serving. How are your endurance levels? If you're struggling, perhaps it's because the work flows not from your walk but from your will. Realigning ourselves with Him first and *then* with His commission makes all the difference when results don't come quickly or easily.

GROUP DISCUSSION

1. How important was Noah's 480 years of walking with God (apparently without any significant "ministry")? What might this say to you?

2. How would you feel if God called you to a ten-year project that everyone around you thought was crazy?

3. The chapter highlighted three elements of Noah's waiting: (1) getting to know God intimately (presence); (2) responding obediently (service); and (3) trusting the Lord's timing. Which of these three is most difficult for you?

4. Barbara Brown Taylor's friend heard the police officer ask, "What made you think that hurrying would help you find your way?" In what area of your own life do you need to slow down?

5. Identify some of the indicators that suggest you might have embraced a vision but not the Visionary.

CHAPTER 2

ABRAHAM: WAIT AND TRUST

*God of comfort who understands my fear and pain, grant me
the strength to wait on you when disappointment or anxiety
threaten to blind me to your Presence. Open my eyes to better
see you and my heart to better trust you. Amen.*

Our faith has to be in the Lord, not in a desired outcome.

Two thousand years before Christ, Abram and Sarai—better
known to us as Abraham and Sarah—waited on God as they walked
a difficult path.

The Bible describes their plight with a single sentence: "Now
Sarai was barren; she had no children" (Genesis 11:30). Any woman
who has suffered infertility—and desired a child—knows that *barren* doesn't begin to describe the experience. Words like *distracted,
preoccupied, emotionally wrung out, and devastated* express the bleakness
a little better. And in the ancient world, a barren woman could

easily find herself discarded by her husband, dealing with the double distress of infertility and the struggle to survive.

"Sarai was barren."

The suffering of the sealed womb has afflicted many women throughout the ages. We can only imagine that Abram and Sarai pleaded with God for a child, just as their son, Isaac, and his wife, Rebekah, would later do (Genesis 25:21), and their grandson Jacob and his wife Rachel would do after them (Genesis 30:22). But Abram and Sarai waited on the Lord during that heartbreak—practicing His Presence, serving Him, and yielding to His timing—a wait that stretched out for many years.

In the midst of that sadness and yearning, God called Abram and Sarai to leave their real estate holdings, to leave their circle of support and influence (their relatives), to leave their future inheritance (their father's house) and "go to the land I will show you. *I will make you into a great nation*" (Genesis 12:1–2). To this barren couple, it might have felt like the last straw. Nothing had worked thus far. The infertility persisted. Sarai did not become pregnant. But perhaps a major act of obedience would open the gates of blessing—and the start of a family.

It doesn't help to psychologize too much about the biblical text, but surely anyone who has walked this pathway of grief can identify with the excitement of God's promise to "make you into a great nation." If obedience to Him would solve the infertility—on a grand scale—you'd be packing your stuff in a heartbeat.

MOVING FROM HARAN

Renowned as a major commercial, cultural, and religious center,[1] Haran (located in today's south-central Turkey) was home to Abram for probably decades as he accumulated wealth, possessions, and servants. Then the Lord came to him and said, "Head on out of here."

We might have responded with a positive commonsense reply: "Sure, Lord. What have you got in mind? Tell me the plan! You know this is no small undertaking, so a little more clarity would help before uprooting everyone and everything." But the New Testament tells us that Abram "obeyed and went, *even though he did not know where he was going*" (Hebrews 11:8). Abram clearly recognized the voice of the Lord (presence) and stepped out in faith (service) even though the Lord had not revealed the whole plan. No crystal balls. No special visions. No advance glimpses. And so at great personal inconvenience and cost—and modeling great obedience—Abram started the trek away from Haran, a place to which he and Sarai would never return.

We don't know how long they traveled, but we know it involved discomfort and danger before they finally settled in Hebron. It also turned into another season to trust the timing of the Lord.

It's hard to lay aside our heart's longing and trust the Lord's goodness.

Over the next eleven years, the Lord spoke to Abram at least three times about having descendants, and having a multitude of them.[2] But still Sarai remained barren. How confusing and frustrating it must have been. It's hard to lay aside our heart's longing and trust the Lord's goodness. It's hard to watch golden opportunities slip away. They did no better than most of us. In desperation, seeing that time was running out, they did what many of us might do. They took matters into their own hands.

The size of the required miracle was growing a little too large for even Abram and Sarai to believe. So in the midst of their quandary, they concocted a plan of their own. Sarai gave her maid, Hagar, to Abram, and Hagar became pregnant. Nine months later, Ishmael was born—outside the preferred plan of God. Then thirteen years passed—nothing from the Lord. No word. No clarification. No affirmation. No promise. No prophecy. And for Sarai, apparently no hope.

But despite all appearances to the contrary, God had not forgotten about Abram and Sarai.

As a ninety-nine-year-old man—nearly twenty-five years after the initial promise—Abram heard the Lord address the issue again:

> "I am God Almighty; walk before me and be blameless. I will confirm my covenant between me and you and will greatly increase your numbers. . . . This is my covenant with you: You will be the father of many nations. No longer will you be called Abram; your name will be Abraham, for I have made you a father of many nations. I will make you very fruitful; I will make nations of you, and kings will come from you."
>
> Genesis 17:1–6

Abram becomes Abraham, and Sarai becomes Sarah. The change of names denoted a change of season and a dramatic turning point in their lives. For twenty-five years they had anticipated "the promise"—trusting but confused; hopeful then discouraged. Now at last, a child (Isaac) was coming.

RECEIVING . . .

The Bible records the birth of Isaac, the promised child, rather matter-of-factly:

> God visited Sarah exactly as he said he would; God did to Sarah what he promised: Sarah became pregnant and gave Abraham a son in his old age, and at the very time God had set. Abraham named him Isaac.
>
> Genesis 21:1–3 THE MESSAGE

Not much more is said. The wait was over. The delighted mother and the doting father no doubt reveled in their newborn. Their gift had arrived. They had waited on God for so long (listening to Him and serving Him)—long enough to lose hope; long enough to give up. But now their promised child had come.

Something happens to us sometimes when God tarries to answer a prayer or fulfill a promise. Subtly, imperceptibly, we fall deeper in love with the promise than with the One who makes the promise. We fantasize about the gift rather than the Giver. We spend so much time imagining what life *will be like* that we fail to live life *as it is.* Our future vision blinds us to our present blessings. It happens all the time.

> *We spend so much time imagining what life* will *be like* that we fail to *live life* as it is.

Recently one of my colleagues was completing his doctorate. The research for his dissertation required him to send out surveys to small cross-sections of students at ten major universities across the United States. It seemed simple enough to his examining committee at the University of North Texas, and they approved his project. But when the time actually came, none of the universities (who had earlier agreed) would proceed. Each insisted that it needed approval from its own Institutional Research Board, and they did not intend to submit his name for approval because he was not one of their students. He had hit the proverbial brick wall.

Chris made phone calls and wrote emails continuously for the first two weeks of October. He contacted everyone from department chairs and international student directors to some of the presidents themselves, but the answer was resolute each time. "No!"

What do you do?

With nowhere else to turn, Chris fell to his knees and prayed for divine intervention. Each night he cried out to the Lord. This project was crucial to completing his doctorate—something he saw as essential for his future. He prayed very specifically, "Lord, I need at least eight universities to participate. The doors are completely closed. And I need them to open by October 31!"

Two things happened. First, and most important, at the end of the third week the Lord performed a miracle. But not the kind you might imagine. The miracle was in Chris's own heart. Like a fresh sea breeze that comes in on a hot summer day, the Spirit of God touched Chris and lifted from him the fear and horror of not being able to complete the doctorate. That dream he had held for so long suddenly took a new perspective. The Spirit gave him a peace beyond his expectation or understanding. Whatever happened after that would be just fine. Life would not end.

Second, in the fourth week of October, permission letters started coming in from the universities. First two, then three, then five—and by October 30, eight! God had performed the seemingly impossible.

As Chris recounted his story to me in early November, he was adamant. As delighted as he felt about the open doors to continue his research, his deepest gratitude centered on the transformation of his heart that the Father had performed. And as he released that which had consumed his heart—and waited on the Lord—he received that which the Father always intended.

Our faith has to be in Him, not in some desired outcome.

Our faith has to be in Him, not in some desired outcome.

Something like this happened with Abraham and Sarah, too. Perhaps over the course of those early years of Isaac's life they had shifted their focus from God to their son. Perhaps they had grown infatuated with their promised child, and their love for the Lord had cooled. The most effective solution for such distraction is often to require the release of what we have received. And so God moved Abraham into a heartrending test.

. . . AND LETTING GO

> Some time later God tested Abraham. He said to him, "Abraham!" "Here I am," he replied. Then God said, "Take your son, your only son, Isaac, whom you love, and go to the region of Moriah. Sacrifice him there as a burnt offering on one of the mountains I will tell you about."
>
> Genesis 22:1–2

Surely not! This son had been given to Abraham and Sarah as a special gift in their old age. And God wanted Abraham to do what? The cruelty of the request seems extraordinary. God had neither required nor even requested this of anyone else in human history.

We might have argued at length, negotiating for our son's freedom. "How about all my herds and flocks instead? How about I build you a special monument? What if I sell everything I have and give it to the poor? Take *me* in his place!" But the Bible tells us that Abraham rose early *the very next morning*, chopped the wood he'd need for this horrible deed, saddled his donkey, and headed out with Isaac (Genesis 22:3). What else could he do as he waited on the Lord? Presence and service, listening and obeying. This was not optional.

"On the third day Abraham looked up and saw the place in the distance" (v. 4). I imagine that for two days he could hardly speak, and when Isaac asked him anything, his replies surely squeezed past a huge lump in his throat. How could he explain this journey to his son? Genesis 22 (NASB) then tells us:

Abraham said to his young men, "Stay here with the donkey, and I and the lad will go over there; and we will worship and return to you."

Abraham took the wood of the burnt offering and laid it on Isaac his son, and he took in his hand the fire and the knife. So the two of them walked on together.

Isaac spoke to Abraham his father and said, "My father!" And he said, "Here I am, my son." And he said, "Behold, the fire and the wood, but where is the lamb for the burnt offering?"

Abraham said, "God will provide for Himself the lamb for the burnt offering, my son." So the two of them walked on together.

Then they came to the place of which God had told him; and Abraham built the altar there and arranged the wood, and bound his son Isaac and laid him on the altar, on top of the wood.

Abraham stretched out his hand and took the knife to slay his son.

vv. 5–10

Abraham had hoped for nearly three days that God would intervene or change His mind—probably the most excruciating three days of Abraham's life. He had no doubt prayed all the way up the mountain and while building the altar. How did he manage to bind his son without a struggle? Where was the lamb for the burnt offering? And in that stunning moment when all seemed lost, Abraham raised his hand to sacrifice his son; his stomach churning, his heart leaping from his chest, his grief about to pour out in torrents.

But the angel of the LORD called to him from heaven and said, "Abraham, Abraham!" And he said, "Here I am."

v. 11 NASB

What an understatement! "Here I am." Surely Abraham was ready to collapse under the burden of this horror. We can imagine his hand barely able to grip the knife, his head swimming and faint. "Here I am" was more likely an explosive "Yes!" He had strained for days to hear from God. He had desperately hoped for a word. And in that near final and fatal moment, it had come.

> He said, "Do not stretch out your hand against the lad, and do nothing to him; for now I know that you fear God, since you have not withheld your son, your only son, from Me."
>
> Then Abraham raised his eyes and looked, and behold, behind him a ram caught in the thicket by his horns; and Abraham went and took the ram and offered him up for a burnt offering in the place of his son.
>
> Abraham called the name of that place The LORD Will Provide, as it is said to this day, "In the mount of the LORD it will be provided."
>
> vv. 12–14 NASB

In her book *When God Is Silent*, Barbara Brown Taylor writes:

> He had passed the test, but Abraham never talked to God again. In the years that were left to him, he spoke *about* God often enough, but he never again spoke *to* God, and God respected the silence. Their conversation was over. Abraham's reward for obeying God's voice was never to have to hear it again.[3]

As Abraham waited on God—living in His Presence and serving Him faithfully—he encountered a divine principle: We must let go of what we love most in order to gain what He wants for us.

OPEN HANDS

We tend to hold on too tightly. Our fixations, fantasies, dreams, and desires become sacrosanct. They may appear honorable and virtuous—a large church, family security, a respectable job, a child—but when they distract us from loving God wholeheartedly they slip from virtue to vice. Our difficulty is in knowing when that transition occurs.

Over time we cease to wait on God; cease to attend or serve Him. He must take a number. Higher priorities demand our attention. It's not that we explicitly reject God. Rather, like the workaholic husband whose marriage collapses without his noticing, we simply drift away from the Lord. And other interests supplant His supremacy in our lives. Biblically speaking, such interests may be defined as idolatrous, and such idolatry has flourished throughout human history.

We must let go of what we love most in order to gain what He wants for us.

Can a promised child—even Isaac—become an idol? Can the honorable cause dishonor within us? Absolutely.

What shall we do?

For Abraham, an outcome of waiting on God meant holding things lightly, not tightly. Waiting on God required trust, even when death itself was just a stroke away. It meant open hands at all times.

The hoarding mentality of our culture—collect, store, and save—undermines our capacity to live with open hands. We like to accumulate and protect. Many garages bulge with unused and unusable items. We jam closets, cupboards, attics, basements, and storage units with more items than we can ever remember, and we get defensive if anyone suggests we get rid of them. Indeed, we arm ourselves heavily to defend ourselves and our possessions.

The U.S. Department of Justice notes:

There are approximately 44 million gun owners in the United States. This means that 25 percent of all adults, and 40 percent of American households, own at least one firearm. These owners possess 192 million firearms. . . . Approximately 37,500 gun sales . . . are completed every day in the United States.[4]

This staggering proliferation of personal firearms—and these statistics date back to 1996—suggests the level of fear that exists in millions of homes across the country. We have grown obsessed with personal safety and protection of our property, and this mindset produces an unhealthy guardedness that keeps us from an open-handed approach to life.

Abraham obviously had an open hand when the Lord called him to move from Haran. He willingly left his comfort and security to obey the leading of God. But when his favored son arrived, his fingers began to curl and his grip strengthened. And the Lord decided to pry those fingers back open.

The same can be true of us. Perhaps it's a career that we always dreamed about that now consumes us. Or the home we always wanted that now sucks up all our God-provided resources. Or that precious vehicle that elicits road rage if anyone threatens to put a scratch on it. Or our own child who should never be blamed, corrected, or criticized. These, and a dozen scenarios like them, illustrate our own inclination to grip rather than give, to seize rather than share.

We cannot wait on God effectively or successfully when our posture is protective. If we want Him to genuinely speak, we must genuinely be willing to release whatever He requests—even our own Isaacs. We must wait and trust.

FULL-TIME FAITH

William Law, an English spiritual writer, wrote in 1728, "Who is the humble, or meek, or devout, or just, or faithful man? Is it he that has several times done acts of humility, meekness, devotion, justice, or fidelity? No; but it is he that lives in *the habitual exercise* of these virtues . . . to the utmost of his power."[5]

William Law spares no one. He insists that those who profess Christ as Lord have a duty to consistency. It's not enough to give occasionally, to be humble periodically, or to show devotion sporadically. Our Lord expects full-time faith. Those who wait on Him must do so at His pleasure (always), not at our whim (periodically).

Those who wait on Him must do so at His pleasure (always), not at our whim (periodically).

In a world of tolerance, backpedaling, soft words, and low expectations, we rarely challenge each other to deeper or greater engagement. We "do not judge so that [we] will not be judged" (Matthew 7:1 NASB). So we justify halfheartedness and excuse lives of convenient commitment.

Perhaps we fail to realize that when we declared, "Christ is Lord," we essentially agreed to surrender *everything* to Him—all our possessions, our time, and our energy, not just a few dollars, a few hours, and a few acts of service.

Such language raises the specter of legalism, and the line is fine indeed. But too often we live in grace and abuse its abundance.

The chaos of creation and the deep brokenness all around us is exacerbated by our apathy and our part-time faith. Not that we utterly neglect doing good and being good. In fine moments we deserve a place among the finest. But until our fine moments become fine lifestyles, we withhold the gospel and the Kingdom from this darkened world.

What might happen if followers of Jesus launched their lives to new levels of trust and loyalty? Never has there been a greater need for full-time faith. It sounds extreme and demanding. The notion of utter self-abandonment and God-trust in every area of our lives sits uneasily amidst the clutter of our comforts and plans. But it reflects the call of Christ to those first disciples, and every disciple since.

Grace does abound for our weakness, fear, and failure. But the cost of our soft grace is paid for by unredeemed, broken, and devastated lives.

Abraham's own story illustrates that nothing can be exempt from this full-time faith journey. We cannot hide a few cherished items for our own discretion. Every gift from God remains His. And the process of learning to wait on the Father (drawing closer to Him and serving Him) requires that we also lay our best and our all on the altar before Him.

WAITING AND THE COVENANT

The result of Abraham's learning to wait on God and trust Him was a covenant of immense proportions. Abraham's obedience has blessed us all. When Abraham untied Isaac with shaking hands and sacrificed the ram the Lord provided, then the Lord said, "All the nations of the earth shall be blessed, *because you have obeyed My voice*" (Genesis 22:18 NASB). Who could have imagined that several thousand years later we would be blessed to walk with the Father, in part because of Abraham's unwavering trust in Him? Jesus, our Savior, came from the line of Abraham through Isaac.

God did not make covenants based on the busyness, ability, or status of people, but rather on their obedience—their willingness to wait on Him. We saw this in the covenant with Noah, and we see it again with Abraham.

What might have happened if Abraham had refused the test with Isaac? What if Abraham and Sarah had been inattentive to the Lord or decided that the cost of serving the Lord was just too high? That waiting on Him was too demanding? They surely would have forfeited the rich blessing God intended for them.

The Father's criteria have remained steady throughout the

ages. His greatest work in the world continues to happen through humble lives yielded and waiting on Him. That's something we all can do. More than that, the covenant promises of the Father continue to find their richest fulfillment in lives that have learned to trust Him most. Waiting on Him, as Abraham shows us, means attentiveness, service, and trust—the kind of trust that releases what we love most in order to accomplish what He desires.

ABRAHAM AND US

When we wait on the Father, we must walk in His Presence with open hands. At times that will require very deep levels of trust. It may also mean letting go of our own dreams so that His purposes can be accomplished. Do we trust His goodness sufficiently to release our dreams into His care?

Perhaps it's a financial dream, a career dream, or a family dream that we have steadily closed our hands around tighter and tighter. Are we willing to release our grip and trust Him for our future? It may feel every bit as painful as the barrenness of Sarai or the Mount Moriah moment of Abraham, but blessing comes to those who wait on the Lord.

The problem many of us face is that we choose to wait for the Lord rather than wait on Him.

Just as Abraham waited on the Lord—listening to Him and responding obediently, even when he couldn't see the end—so must we. The problem many of us face is that we choose to wait *for* the Lord rather than wait *on* Him. We keep waiting for Him to lead in certain ways, do certain things, and provide certain blessings. We bide time waiting *for* Him rather than spend our lives waiting *on* Him. As table waiters to the Lord, our life's journey may still have its bumps and bruises, its hurts and disappointments, but as we resolve to trust

Him implicitly, the fullness of life transcends the fears and frustrations that threaten to overtake us.

Abraham's story calls us to deep trust in the plan, the provision, and the promises of God. Do we have that trust?

GROUP DISCUSSION

1. Why might the Lord have had Abraham and Sarah wait twenty-five years to fulfill His promise of a son (Isaac)?

2. Describe a time when you fantasized more about the gift (what you were waiting for) than the Giver. Did you have to let go of the dream before you could encounter God in the deeper places?

3. What does it take to live with "open hands"? How do you rise above the temptation to hold tight to what you have?

4. Waiting on the Lord demands full surrender of our possessions, our time, and our energy; not just a few dollars, a few hours, and a few acts of service. What might this mean for your life?

5. Abraham and Sarah learned to trust the Lord as they waited on Him. On a scale of 1–10 (where 1 is dismal and 10 is extraordinary), what's your level of trust in God today? What would it take for you to move that up one notch?

CHAPTER 3

MOSES: WAIT AND LEARN

Father, you who guide me and sustain me through the wilderness, open my eyes to see more than my own circumstances and to see your hand directing the larger picture of my life. I trust you with it—entirely. Amen.

At the 2008 *ReThink Conference*, Robert Schuller Jr., from the Crystal Cathedral in Garden Grove, California, was discussing the new ways that people find marriage partners and build relationships in this electronic world. He mentioned a good friend of his who "found his wife on eBay." Schuller meant to say eHarmony, and we all chuckled at the slip of the tongue. We could just picture the frantic (or slow) bidding for a marriage partner as the clock ticked down online. Perhaps this would appeal to the impatient or impulsive among us who have no time for dating!

IMPULSIVE

Moses apparently had an impulsive streak in him. He was born of a Hebrew woman who then hid him in a wicker basket to escape Pharaoh's death decree against all Hebrew baby boys. Through God's miraculous intervention, Moses was raised by his mother *and Pharaoh's own daughter.* Yet we know virtually nothing of Moses' early life, except that he enjoyed privilege and grew up in the lap of luxury.

The Bible picks up his story when he is forty years old and details an impulsive incident that would turn his life upside-down.

> One day, after Moses had grown up, he went out to where his own people were and watched them at their hard labor. He saw an Egyptian beating a Hebrew, one of his own people. Glancing this way and that and seeing no one, he killed the Egyptian and hid him in the sand.
>
> Exodus 2:11–12

What was Moses thinking? Egyptians beat Hebrews every day. Slaves expected it and taskmasters delivered it. Many had suffered beatings before that day, and many would endure them after it. But in an impulsive moment Moses decided he would step in and protect his fellow Hebrew. Was it compassion or rage that drove him? Had he premeditated the act or been driven by a spontaneous fury? We don't know. But somewhere deep inside Moses stirred a sense of justice—perhaps something planted within him many years earlier by his Jewish mother. At forty years of age, he had seen enough. And he met violence with violence.

The brutal slaying of Kitty Genovese shocked New York City in 1964. Late at night, with only streetlights piercing the darkness, her assailant pursued and attacked her three separate times over thirty-five minutes in her high-density neighborhood. He finally stabbed her to death on the narrow front porch of a house just up the street from her own home. But something more horrifying overshadowed the sickening violence. Detectives later determined that thirty-eight of Kitty's neighbors had watched her ordeal from their windows and not a single person had come out or called for help.[1]

Psychologists subsequently coined the phrase *The Genovese Syndrome* to describe the shocking paralysis that people sometimes experience when witnessing violence. They concluded that when many people are present, we are less likely to respond. The smaller the group of onlookers, the higher the likelihood that someone will take action in a crisis or emergency.

Moses had glanced to the left and right and seen no one else watching—or perhaps no one else available to help—so he killed the Egyptian.

> The next day he went out and saw two Hebrews fighting. He asked the one in the wrong, "Why are you hitting your fellow Hebrew?"
>
> The man said, "Who made you ruler and judge over us? Are you thinking of killing me as you killed the Egyptian?" Then Moses was afraid and thought, "What I did must have become known."
>
> When Pharaoh heard of this, he tried to kill Moses, but Moses fled from Pharaoh and went to live in Midian.
>
> Exodus 2:13–15

Moses' life of luxury and affluence came to an abrupt end. Nobody, not even a prince of Egypt, could arbitrarily kill another Egyptian in defense of a slave. Moses, the privileged and adopted son of Pharaoh's daughter, became a wanted man. In a flash, he fell from power to poverty. With little more than the clothes on his back, he fled for his life across the Sinai Peninsula (where Israel would later encamp for forty years) to the land of Midian, far to the east. Surely that put him beyond the reach of the supreme ruler of Egypt. And there he remained, a subdued radical.

RADICAL FAITH

Conferences and seminars today routinely challenge young people to do something radical for Christ. That might mean prayer-walking the cities of South America, rescuing refugees in Africa, or joining inner-city communes or monastic-like orders to reach the homeless and the hurting.

This defines *radical Christianity*, we're told. The most radical people are those who do the wildest, most unexpected, most dangerous things.

I would not want to diminish these honorable pursuits for a moment. But truly radical Christianity is not defined by geographical locations or external circumstances. Radical Christianity is the complete and utter surrender of our own will to the will of God. Nothing is more radical, extreme . . . or rare. Sacred waiting is radical Christianity.

Motivational speakers, pumping up crowds and pounding podiums, often advocate a kind of cowboy Christianity that appeals especially to men: "A few good men." "The few, the proud, and the brave." Ironically, the pursuit of world change can be self-serving and self-honoring. In some instances, as wowed audiences applaud our stories of sacrifice, danger, and adventure (for Christ), we plan the next foray much the way that an addict plans his next fix. Spiritual heroism may feed our own need for significance more than reflect lives humbly offered to Christ and lived out of the deep security we have in Him and our unwavering commitment to wait at His table.

What constitutes radical Christianity? The genuinely, constantly, and deeply yielded heart that is shaped by time in His Presence and by service to His leading.

The college student who volunteers at the local nursing home; the teenager who tutors the struggling middle-schooler; the mom who serves as a spiritual friend to many who call her; the man who funds mission trips for others. Each of these can express more radical Christianity than many of the glory stories that hit platforms and publications, especially if they arise from sacred waiting.

> *Radical Christianity is the complete and utter surrender of our own will to the will of God.*

The issue is not what we *do,* but what motivates us. The most extreme acts of service become ordinary in God's sight when they come from a self-honoring heart. Conversely, our unnoticed deeds become radical when they reflect deep, selfless obedience to Christ.

The word *radical* originally referred to "that which comes from the roots." We measure it, therefore, not by one's actions, but by one's motives. We model truly radical Christianity when we move beyond the flashy exterior of our faith and pursue complete yieldedness of heart. That yieldedness generally arises from practicing the Presence of God, a discipline for which we are poorly trained.

We might prophesy, cast out demons, perform many miracles in His name—or even kill an oppressive Egyptian taskmaster—but such things do little to impress the Lord. Instead, the gates of heaven swing open for those "who [do] the will of My Father who is in heaven" (Matthew 7:21 NASB).

We might surmise that in his exile, Moses began to learn these truths. He began to learn that impulsiveness—taking charge of something that God already has under control—does not achieve the purposes of the Lord. Moses began to learn that serving the people of God means partnership with God.

THE BURNING BUSH

Once Moses arrived in his remote hideaway, a season of forty years passed, and once again we know surprisingly little about it, except that Moses married a local girl (Zipporah) and had a son (Gershom). He spent those four decades as a shepherd living quietly without any other purpose, focus, direction, or calling than to wait on God. Until the day he came to Horeb, the mountain of the Lord.[2]

Moses had lived a life in two halves. For forty years he enjoyed education, power, wealth, and privilege. And for forty years he endured the blistering heat and bone-chilling cold of the wilderness as he watched flocks in silence and solitude. Alfred Delp once wrote: "The desert is not a place of refuge or a value in itself. Instead, it is a place of preparation, of waiting, of readiness, of listening for the word of commission."[3]

So who could forget that day? Burning but not burned; on fire but untouched. The bush caught Moses' attention, and as he approached it to take a closer look, the Lord said, "Do not come any closer.... Take off your sandals, for the place where you are standing is holy ground" (Exodus 3:5). Moses found himself in the very Presence of God.

In the conversation that followed, the Lord put His plan to Moses in straightforward terms. "Go back to Egypt, speak with Pharaoh, and bring My people out of the land" (see v. 10).

"Oh, right! Lord, if you wanted me to save Israel, why didn't you get behind me forty years ago when I was young, strong, and willing? Why did you tarry until now? I've lost my bravado, my strength, my confidence, and even my ability to speak clearly!"

The Bible doesn't record these words of Moses, but he surely thought it if he didn't say it. In short, Moses had gone from forty-year-old arrogance to eighty-year-old anxiety—just what the Lord wanted.

For forty years Moses had *un*learned his self-assurance and his personal dreams. He had learned to shepherd in the wilderness rather than issue edicts from the royal palace. He had tuned his ear to the voice of God rather than the voice of culture. Now, at eighty years of age, Moses stood physically weaker, materially empty-handed, emotionally less self-assured, and rightly prepared for God to use him. He had learned to release his personal ambition, to shift his focus from the plight of his circumstances to the privilege of God's Presence, and to crucify his elitism and embrace humility. The harshness of the desert had reconfigured Moses' priorities, softened his self-confidence, and finally molded him to wait authentically on the Lord.

WAIT AND LEARN

During my college experience, my professors downloaded amazing amounts of information and tested their students often to see if what was pouring from the jug was making it to the mug. I graduated with reams of paper covered with hand-written notes. Those notes filled binders, and those binders filled shelves. According to my college, after four years I was educated. And I felt a strong urgency to get out and pass on the knowledge I had acquired. It felt good to know so much of what I had never known before, and I felt sure that if others knew it, they'd feel good, too. Of course, I've long since forgotten much of it, which makes Google such a godsend!

Moses' forty years in the wilderness provided a learning experience of a very different kind. The desert became his classroom, and solitude became his tutor. He did not race through a four-year baccalaureate program or grapple with letter grades or GPAs. He did not arrive at the burning bush (his graduation moment) with loads of data or a neat systematic theology. Nor did he stand before the Lord with a polished skill set or good answers to tough questions. Not at all.

If Moses had learned anything to speak of, he had learned to be still. The desert had tempered his impetuosity, impatience, and self-reliance. Now he had learned patience, humility, and dependence. Nobody survives in the wilderness on their own. His faith in himself had turned to faith in the Lord. The writer to the Hebrews tells us that Moses left Egypt and "persevered because he saw him who is invisible" (Hebrews 11:27). He learned to see the hand of God where once he had seen only his own hand. The harsh landscape had recharged his vision. The arid conditions sharpened his survival skills and nurtured a divine thirst in his soul.

Forty years is a long time to learn these lessons. Some of us may have counted off each year, wondering when we would be launched into something significant; when we might receive "our call" to change the world. But the forty years gradually worked that false expectation out of Moses' system. This wilderness experience was not just a parole period before he could be set free to achieve some grand design. Moses learned that the wilderness may *be* his life calling. Waiting on God—presence and service—is not the means to another end, not a trade-off for a special commission. To be present for Christ and responsive to His requests, however large or small, must be privilege enough. And this seeped deeply into Moses.

> *Waiting on God is not the means to another end, not a trade-off for a special commission.*

We have no indication from the Bible that Moses begged the Lord at the end of each passing year for some great task, as though his life felt squandered or wasted in shepherding. He might have complained that the Lord was underutilizing his leadership abilities and education. He could have grown bitter that his unique potential lay untapped. But nothing in the biblical text suggests such arrogance.

When the Lord spoke from the burning bush, Moses did not reply with a sigh of relief: "At last! I wondered how long before I got a serious call!" On the contrary, he hesitated, unsure that he was even the man for the job. Yet while he may have lost confidence in his own abilities, he did not lose confidence in the Lord.

I'M READY

In 1982, I found myself working for the National Australia Bank, saving hard to travel to the United States for two years to get some college classes that could start me off as a preacher. In my youthful ignorance and enthusiasm, I had dismissed the idea of a full college degree. What I needed, I concluded, were some Bible classes and a couple of preaching courses. Then I could return to Australia and jump into ministry. I wanted an Egyptian crash course, not a Midianite wilderness experience.

These many years later—and three degrees later—I'm a little surprised; not at my immature approach to education but by the fact that most of my studies neglected the training I needed the most. Nothing surpasses the desert for depth of learning. And authentic leadership must never be reduced to creative ideas, clever speech, or high energy levels. If we have anything to say or any commission to fulfill or any purpose to pursue, it must ultimately come from the deep wells of Midian and an encounter at Horeb—or Calvary— not the springs of the Nile delta. Calling comes not because of our abilities but because we have ears that hear Christ.

Sacred waiting means living lives attentive to God while at the same time crucifying our visions of personal significance and competence. Sacred waiting calls us to look for the burning bush, however long it takes, and not create a burning bush of our own, even if no burning bush ever appears. Sacred waiting recognizes the immaturity of impetuosity and embraces contentment—even when the Lord's timing sometimes leaves us feeling forgotten. Sacred waiting thrusts us into tasks of service that the Lord designs, not a ministry of our own making.

NEVER OVERLOOKED

Have you ever felt overlooked by God? Ever felt that you have spent too long in a remote place and He must have forgotten you? Ever wondered if the Lord has dumped you in the dry desert as punishment rather than preparation? Ever wondered if you might have missed the boat, grown too old, or failed the test?

Perhaps part of our struggle comes from our own expectations, which blind us to the Lord's invitation.

In *Abba's Child*, Brennan Manning tells a powerful story that deserves repetition:

> Thornton Wilder's one-act play "The Angel That Troubled the Waters" [1928], based on John 5:1–4, dramatizes the power of the pool of Bethesda to heal whenever an angel stirred its waters. A physician comes periodically to the pool hoping to be the first in line and longing to be healed of his melancholy. The angel finally appears but blocks the physician just as he is ready to step into the water. The angel tells the physician to draw back, for this moment is not for him. The physician pleads for help in a broken voice, but the angel insists that healing is not intended for him.
>
> The dialogue continues—and then comes the prophetic word from the angel: "Without your wounds where would your power be? It is your melancholy that makes your low voice tremble into the hearts of men and women. The very angels themselves cannot persuade the wretched and blundering children on earth as can one human being broken on the wheels of living. In Love's service, only wounded soldiers can serve. Physician, draw back."
>
> Later, the man who enters the pool first and is healed rejoices in his good fortune and turning to the physician says: "Please come with me. It is only an hour to my home. My son is lost in dark thoughts. I do not understand him and only you have ever lifted his mood. Only an hour. . . . There is also my daughter: since her child died, she sits in the shadow. She will not listen to us but she will listen to you." [4]

As we pray for healing and yearn to be first into "the troubled waters," are we aware of those in the shadows to whom the Father may send us? Ultimately, in a broken world our healing is less helpful than our woundedness. Our pain, in His hands, can "tremble into the hearts of men and women" and, miraculously, become a balm as it connects us together and opens opportunities to share a higher vision.

Henri Nouwen, in his classic work *The Wounded Healer,* expresses words that ring true for all of us when he says, "A Christian community is . . . a healing community not because wounds are cured and pains are alleviated, but because wounds and pains become openings or occasions for a new vision."[5]

Our grief, pain, brokenness, and sorrow all have transforming power in the hands of the real Physician. We sometimes see them as impediments to ministry. He sees them as foundational. We want to move on, but perhaps He says, "Draw back." Our hearts and our hurts generally provide far richer material for Christ to use than our skills or talents. Perhaps we need to adjust our perspective.

Some of us, at times, know exactly how we expect Christ to use us and His delay deeply frustrates us. But like Moses—and the physician in Wilder's one-act play—we might do well to embrace His direction. Sacred waiting demands it.

WAITING AND THE COVENANT

Just like Noah and Abraham, Moses learned to wait on God over an extended period of time, and then the Lord established a major covenant with His people. Not only did He use Moses to deliver the people of Israel from their Egyptian bondage, but as the nation passed by Horeb again during its wilderness wanderings, God took the opportunity to establish a covenant with them that would affect us all.

How must Moses have felt? The last time on Horeb he'd been

herding a small flock of sheep and goats in search of water and feed, and then seen the remarkable burning bush. Now he found himself leading a couple of million people in the same region.

Perhaps Moses remembered the exact place where he saw the burning bush. Did he quietly slip out of the Israelite camp by night to secretly check if the bush still remained? Who knows? But the bush had served its purpose and no longer glowed. Yet Moses would encounter the Lord again on Horeb, repeatedly.

The book of Exodus details for us that Moses made multiple trips up and down Mount Sinai (also known as Mount Horeb) while the people of Israel camped down below, forbidden to even touch the mountain (Exodus 19:12). At times various leaders of Israel accompanied Moses partway up the mountain, but ultimately the Lord said to Moses, "Come up to me on the mountain and stay here, and I will give you the tablets of stone, with the law and commands I have written for their instruction" (Exodus 24:12).

> And the glory of the LORD settled on Mount Sinai. For six days the cloud covered the mountain, and on the seventh day the LORD called to Moses from within the cloud. To the Israelites the glory of the LORD looked like a consuming fire on top of the mountain. Then Moses entered the cloud as he went on up the mountain. And he stayed on the mountain forty days and forty nights.
>
> Exodus 24:16–18

While Moses waited on the Lord, the people of Israel did not. They built their golden calf and worshiped it at the base of the mountain on which God himself rested. And it kindled God's anger such that He threatened to destroy Israel (Exodus 32:10). Thankfully, the Lord relented, and Moses spent another forty days and nights on the mountaintop as the Lord rewrote the words of the covenant (Exodus 34:28), which included promises and blessings for the people of Israel.

Could God not have given the written covenant to Moses when He first spoke to him through the burning bush? Why the lengthy process? Why the delay?

God's blessings, like His special covenants at various times throughout human history, always arrive in His timing. And that timing inevitably teaches us a great deal about Him, and ourselves.

MOSES AND US

Sacred waiting is never time wasted, or time lost. Rather, like seasoning, it reflects time that teaches us and matures us. In our seasons of wilderness wanderings, we have no promise that a burning bush awaits us in the end, or that glory, prominence, and importance—highly valued by our culture—will follow. Instead, we have the greater promise. The promise that even on an arid mountainside and a barren mountaintop, the Lord is present. Will we be fully present with Him?

Moses had a great deal to *un*learn as he waited on God in the wilderness. We might imagine all the hyphenated self sins (self-importance, self-assurance, self-confidence, self-justification, self-service) and more. Perhaps God intends waiting to be a formative season of *un*learning and *re*learning for us, too.

> *Sacred waiting is never time wasted, or time lost.*

We see the struggles, hurts, and needs around us, and want to take charge. We feel indignant at the injustice and oppression rampant in the world and resolve to tackle it aggressively. But the Father has much to teach us first, not least of all that He is sovereign and we are not. As we wait on the Lord through what may feel like dry and parched times, will it evolve into a sacred wait: presence, then service?

Most important, will we wait on the Lord if it means wilderness wandering for the rest of our lives? That's precisely what it became for Moses.

GROUP DISCUSSION

1. Describe a time when you had a "wilderness wandering," if you've had one. How did it shape you?

2. "Our unnoticed deeds become radical when they reflect deep, selfless obedience to Christ." Why do we often struggle to be content with unnoticed deeds of faith? And in what sense might your unnoticed deeds be more radical than some of the highly visible "acts of faith"?

3. What strikes you most about Moses' learning experience in Midian? After that education, what traits do you think most qualified him to lead Israel out of Egypt? How does this compare with your view of preparation for ministry or service?

4. "Our hearts and our hurts generally provide far richer material for Christ to use than our skills or talents." How has the Lord used your hurt or woundedness to better minister to others? Why do you think He works most powerfully this way?

5. What do you think changed Moses' wilderness experience from simply "biding time" into "sacred waiting"?

CHAPTER 4

DAVID: WAIT AND WORSHIP

Father, above all else that is happening in my life, help me to see you. Shift my focus from demanding my own agenda to worshiping you. Teach me to be more fully present to your Presence. May waiting and worshiping form the bedrock of my life. Amen.

We live in a ruined world. The chaos, carnage, and corruption staggers the mind. With violence at every turn and heartbreak in every corner, the extent of the need overwhelms some people while it motivates others. Newscasts carry images of young girls on the streets of Southeast Asia, serving a male tourist trade. Mission agencies show photographs of AIDS orphans, now numbering millions throughout Africa. Bombings and shootings span the globe from Iraq to downtown Los Angeles. Emaciated bodies pick through garbage dumps in Mexico, looking for scraps to eat. Drug cartels intimidate communities and cities around the world. And then natural disasters—hurricanes, earthquakes, fires, and floods—randomly destroy thousands of lives. What can we do?

Eugene Peterson, author of *The Message*, notes that we can adopt a Greek or a Hebrew approach to the crises that surround us.

> The Hebrews were not so much interested in understanding the human condition as they were in responding to the divine reality. Their supreme effort was to hear God's word, not to tell stories about gods. Their characteristic speech form was not the myth but the prayer. They were deeply committed to a way of life that pivoted on the acts of God.
>
> There *was* something to be done about the human condition, but it was not primarily what men and women attempted but what God is doing. In order to get in on that action they prayed. Their purpose was not to understand what was going on in the human race but to be a part of what was going on with God. The Greeks were experts on understanding existence from a human point of view; the Hebrews were experts in setting human existence in response to God. Whereas the Greeks had a story for every occasion, the Hebrews had a prayer for every occasion.[1]

The distinction between these two worldviews is enormous. The Hebrew model starts with God; the Greek model starts with us.

Consider the phenomenon of the sun rising each morning. For centuries, with no other perspective than that of a person standing and watching the sunrise, men and women assumed that the sun rotated around the earth. It seemed obvious. That huge glowing ball came up over the horizon in the morning, crossed the sky during the day, and dropped out of sight in the evening. Since we could not feel any movement on our part, the sun was clearly moving around us. Until Copernicus suggested otherwise less than five hundred years ago.[2]

Because we could not find an external vantage point (away from the planet) to see what was really happening, we assumed that the entire universe revolved around us. This represents the

Greek approach to life. Everything starts with humanity as the basic reference point. But the Hebrew view of life and reality starts with a different fixed point: God.

As Christians, when we begin to grasp these two different starting points for interpreting the events of the world, we realize the importance of the psalms. These prayerful songs of ancient Israel have suffered routine neglect among Christians, for various reasons. On the one hand, they belong to the Old Testament, and we commonly assume that

> *The Hebrew view of life and reality starts with a different fixed point: God.*

they have little relevance to a New Covenant people. We prefer the Gospels and Paul's letters. Besides, talk about sacrifices, the temple, and the Law seems hard to translate into our contemporary setting. On the other hand, the poetic language of the psalms fails to appeal to most of us who live predominantly with a left-brained, rationalist worldview. Many of us prefer bullet points over repetitious couplets or seemingly redundant parallelisms. Consequently the psalms fall quickly into disuse.

The psalms do not provide a systematic theology in the sense that they neatly progress from one truth to another, building a watertight system of thought. Yet at the same time, they reflect a deep commitment to several basic themes that recur with great consistency. And prominent among those themes is the affirmation that sacred waiting—waiting on the Lord—brings all of life into a new perspective. It enables us to approach poverty and prosperity, suffering and success, anxiety and comfort, pain and pleasure, fear and faith from a different, more life-giving vantage point: the high ground of worship.

King David stands out as chief among the psalmists who wait and worship.

KING DAVID

Among all of Israel's military and political leaders, none has so revered a place as the ancient King David. Ruling a thousand years before the coming of Jesus, he expanded the influence and control of Israel farther than King Saul before him and any king after him. His reign became the golden era of Israel's history. He led great conquests and accumulated enormous wealth, but he also experienced prolonged seasons of uncertainty in his own life, seasons sometimes marked by fear, anxiety, grief, and distress.

As a young man, the youngest of eight brothers, he learned patience, courage, faith, music—and to wait on the Lord—while shepherding sheep for his father. His home was not a palace but the hills around Bethlehem. He had no dreams of greatness, and no one else apparently had dreams of greatness for him. But in the fields and with the flocks he experienced the Presence of God and quietly served the Lord.

When Samuel the prophet came looking to anoint a successor to Saul (see 1 Samuel 16), David's father, Jesse, paraded his seven oldest sons before the prophet and didn't even consider David worth calling in from the pastures. But the Lord appointed David—young, untrained in army warfare, uneducated in politics—and Samuel anointed him.

It's difficult to calculate the time span between David's anointing by Samuel and his coronation as successor to King Saul, but we ought to measure it in many years—at least a decade or more.

David's story, as he followed the leading of the Lord, had constant twists and turns. As a young man, when he took food to his brothers in battle, he found himself confronting and killing Israel's #1 enemy, Goliath. King Saul was there and later invited David to the palace to play his harp when Saul felt troubled in spirit (1 Samuel 16:18–19). Then he became one of Saul's armor-bearers (v. 21). David grew in popularity with the people, and Saul grew in jealousy. Thereafter, David survived several savage attacks on his life by the king. He was reduced in military honor, cheated of his promised bride (the daughter of the king), and finally set to flight by the relentless (and violent) Saul. No place remained safe for long, and those who helped David were sometimes cruelly punished by the rage-maddened king (1 Samuel 22:6–19)—prophets, priests, and national enemies alike. Twice when David had opportunity to kill the king and seize the throne for which Samuel had anointed him years before, he spared the life of Saul (1 Samuel 24, 26). All the while, he trusted the Lord's timing and protection.

Finally, after the death of Saul in another battle against the Philistines, the men of Judah came and confirmed David as king. He was thirty years old, and spent the first two years of his reign battling with old supporters of Saul. Just when he might have expected the doors to swing wide open and the Lord to catapult him into fame and success, David found himself still trusting the Lord's timing as he faced staunch opposition. And during each stage of his life he continued to wait on the Lord—presence and service—as he had learned while a young shepherd.

The privileged reign of King David over thirty-five years did not spare him the "stuff" of life—the heartaches, the failures, the sin, and the uncertainty. The palace may have provided a comfortable bed, but he spent many a night tossing, turning, and even weeping (see Psalm 55:17). Servants may have attended his every demand, but he quickly learned that God was not one of his servants. The glory he experienced in worldly terms did not qualify him for special exemptions in the Lord's sight. David's rule could never supplant the sovereignty of God, and thus he, like us, had to wait on the Lord.

THE PSALMS

The most consistent windows we have into the life of David are not the stories retold by the ancient historians, but the psalms that he wrote. While David's life contained multiple stories of heroism, courage, valor, and political intrigue, his worship life reveals another side of him. The shepherd boy harpist, who evidently wrote many songs that became popular worship anthems, expressed his heart most fully not in battle but with poetry and music.

While we struggle to date all of the psalms that David wrote, and no doubt have only a few of his original pieces,[3] what we have reveals something fundamental about David's faith journey and his view of waiting on God. Over the years, he evidently learned to wait on the Lord not only as an act of obedience and patience, but above all, worship. Little wonder then that for three millennia the psalms have provided the people of God with raw material for worship.

As we read the laments and the honest cries of the psalmist, we realize that waiting on God is both universal and difficult. In the midst of life's challenges—when enemies seem to prevail, when a child dies, when fear rushes at us, when we feel betrayed or abandoned, when we hurt others in ways we never intended—waiting on God feels almost impossible. The Lord can feel so distant and serving Him can feel pointless, especially when He remains silent. Yet David consistently turned again to the Lord and worshiped Him. When we experience pain and fear, surely He should jump to our aid, and quickly. Like a doting Father, surely He should even anticipate our hardships and intervene to prevent them. And when He fails to minimize our conflict or loss, it confuses or upsets us. At precisely such times, the psalms serve us well. They methodically turn our attention away from the circumstances of life that we see and turn us toward the reality of God's Presence and provision. But the psalms also call us to lift our sights above the horizon of our circumstances. Rather than being absorbed by the trouble and threats around us, the psalms repeatedly enjoin us to wait on the Lord. They call us to lives of sacred waiting that become lives of worship.

> In the morning, O LORD, you hear my voice; in the morning
> I lay my requests before you and *wait* in expectation.
>
> Psalm 5:3

David's prayerful attentiveness to God does not end with the *amen*. Rather, having laid out his requests, he continues to watch and see throughout the day how the Lord may choose to answer; not simply because he is hopeful of getting his way, but because he wants to see the hand of God and then respond appropriately to it. This often provides the crucial difference between David's waiting and our own. The term translated *wait* has the sense of looking and watching, not checking back in at a later time.[4] Our prayerfulness frequently falls short of this "waiting in expectation."

> Indeed, none of those who *wait* for You will be ashamed. . . .
> You are the God of my salvation; for You I *wait* all the day.
>
> Psalm 25:3, 5 NASB

This psalm drives the point home even deeper.[5] Throughout the Psalm, David looks back on his own sin and setbacks, yet expresses his unwavering confidence in the grace of God. And he finds himself grounded once again in the powerful Presence of God, exalting the Lord for his salvation. This exaltation and constant attentiveness helps define worship. Even when David is not sure of his next step or is ashamed of his past, he turns repeatedly to the Lord: waiting on Him, worshiping Him.

Waiting on the Father ought to

> *We bring Him our sin, our sorrow, and our setbacks. And He affirms our salvation.*

elicit such times of worship from us, too. As we turn to the Father and "wait all the day," we bring Him our sin, our sorrow, and our setbacks. And He affirms our salvation. Then we, like David, grow in hope.

WAITING WITH HOPE

We typically think of hope as wishful thinking. "I hope God answers my prayer." "I hope it works out all right for you." "I hope I can go." But this tentativeness distorts the solid hope of the psalmist and the hope that we should have as followers of Christ.

Thomas Merton, a Trappist monk who wrote extensively on the deeper spiritual life, concluded: "We can either love God because we hope for something from Him, or we can hope in Him knowing that He loves us."[6] The difference between the two positions is enormous. When we love God in an effort to solicit His favor, we always have a level of uncertainty. Will He see it the way I do? Will I catch Him in a generous mood? Is this too much to ask? How does He feel about me today? Ultimately, this kind of hope is riddled with doubt and various levels of anxiety. It also leads to disappointment and frustration when God fails to deliver what we expect. Indeed, when we place our hope in anything or anyone other than God himself, we almost inevitably turn against God for letting us down in some way. "I deserved to keep my job." "I deserved to have a baby." "I deserved to recover from cancer." The outcome is often bitterness. But this turns the whole table waiter metaphor backwards. We approach the Lord only so that He can attend to us and serve our needs. Thus, when our hope rests in what He can do for us rather than in who He is to us, it is misguided.

The hope that we have as followers of Jesus is not speculative or wishful. It has nothing to do with specific responses that we expect from the Father. Its sole foundation is a resolute and unshakable confidence in the love of God for us. With such conviction, nothing else matters. Everything else is, at best, temporary. We can't "lose" anything because we don't hold tightly to any*thing* or claim any*thing* or hope in any*thing*. We hold tightly only to Him. Our lives then become genuine acts of worship. Our waiting on Christ becomes an expression of single-minded love and devotion.

When our hope rests in what He can do for us rather than in who He is to us, it is misguided.

Thus the psalmist shows us an entirely different kind of hope. It's grounded not in the flimsy, wishful thinking of the world but in an unwavering confidence in the Father's love. When our hope rests solely and fully in the Father's unquenchable love for us, nothing else in life controls us. We can release our grasp on everything because we find ourselves smitten by the only certain thing that matters—His love. And as we release our grip, the Lord is free to gently fill our open hands with more than we ever imagined.

Here's the tremendous paradox that the psalmist highlights for us: As we wait on the Lord, we release all else and thereby enable the Lord to give us all things, which we receive authentically not in ownership but as stewardship. We don't wait on Him in order to receive, as though we could use sacred waiting to manipulate Him in any way. That type of waiting is corrupt and polluted with self-serving motives and a faithless agenda. But we wait on the Father because we have a solid hope in Him through Christ. And the fruit of such waiting is worship. As we stand in His Presence and serve Him, we find ourselves bowed in worship and wonder.

The apostle Paul reflected this confidence, this hope, when he wrote:

Who shall separate us from *the love of Christ*? Shall trouble or hardship or persecution or famine or nakedness or danger or sword? . . . No, in all these things we are more than conquerors through him *who loved us*. For I am convinced that neither death nor life, neither angels nor demons, neither the present nor the future, nor any powers, neither height nor depth, nor anything else in all creation, will be able to separate us from *the love of God that is in Christ Jesus our Lord*.

Romans 8:35, 37–39

Waiting on God reflects our confidence in Him as well as builds our confidence in Him. It only happens when we move from fanciful thinking to worship, and from uncertainty to clarity about what matters most—His unstoppable and unconquerable love for each of us. Therefore, the psalmist can write: "We wait in hope for the LORD; he is our help and our shield" (Psalm 33:20).

WAITING AND WORSHIP

Our understanding of worship may need a major restructuring. The daily devotional, if practiced at all, usually gets a few minutes of early morning energy or late night exhaustion, and weekend worship services have tended far more toward performances that we watch or rituals that we mindlessly repeat, arriving on "church time" (five or ten minutes late), and then watching the clock to ensure we can get to our local restaurant before the crowds do.

Scripture, however, constantly affirms that worship is a verb, not a noun. It is something we do, not something we sit through; something that engages us, not something that we watch. The biblical view of worship sees it as a lifestyle rather than an isolated act. Paul wrote, "Therefore, I urge you, brothers, in view of God's mercy, to offer your bodies as living sacrifices, holy and pleasing to God—this is your spiritual act of worship" (Romans 12:1).

True worship involves offering ourselves as living and constant sacrifices. Such worship means that everything we do reflects our love for the Lord, our desire for intimacy with Him, and our willingness to serve His cause. Serving the poor, coaching Little League, watching a movie, listening to the radio, cooking a meal, working on the job, raising children, and loving a marriage partner can all be acts of worship that come from waiting on the Lord. And each activity or experience turns into an act of worship as we practice sacred waiting—giving specific attention to Christ by doing all things as unto Him. "Whatever you do, whether in word or deed, do it all in the name of the Lord Jesus, giving thanks to God the Father through him" (Colossians 3:17).

Throughout his life, David also understood that waiting, living, and worshiping are all connected. Sacred waiting—worshipful waiting—reflects a lifestyle of attentiveness; not simply in times of distress or grief but in all circumstances.

> *Wait* for the LORD; be strong and take heart and *wait* for the LORD.
>
> Psalm 27:14

> *Wait* for the LORD and keep his way.
>
> Psalm 37:34

> I *wait* for you, O LORD; you will answer, O Lord my God.
>
> Psalm 38:15

> I *waited* patiently for the LORD; he turned to me and heard my cry.
>
> Psalm 40:1

> I will *wait* on Your name, for it is good.
>
> Psalm 52:9 NASB

David composed these psalms during various phases of his life; times of joy and times of fear, times of celebration and times of discouragement. Yet amidst it all, he identified worship as intrinsic to waiting on the Lord. Time after time, despite the circumstances, David reminded himself (and us) of the sovereignty of God and resolved to wait on Him with a worshipful heart.

How many of us share this perspective of waiting on the Lord? Noah waited and endured; Abraham waited and trusted; Moses waited and learned; David waited and worshiped. Indeed, David learned that whether you're watching sheep, facing giants, running for your life, or leading a nation, God's Presence is the bottom line. It never changes. He never changes. Thus whatever our status or standing in life, we're called to worship. Do we share such devotion?

We set deadlines for answers from God, and as those deadlines draw closer—without clarity as to what we should do—we tend to grow in one of two ways. We either grow impatient or we grow prayerful. We either grow more demanding or more trusting. We find ourselves driven to anxiety or to worship. The psalmist found that waiting on the Lord taught him to worship more authentically and consistently. Is that true for us?

WAITING AND THE COVENANT

God's covenant with David stands out as one of the major covenants in the Old Testament. Just as He established major covenants with Noah, Abraham, and Moses, so the Lord also made a unilateral promise to David.

> "I have made a covenant with my chosen one, I have sworn to David my servant, I will establish your line forever and make your throne firm through all generations."
>
> Psalm 89:3–4

God promised to establish the throne of David forever. The "house of David" would never disappear. And God fulfilled this promise perfectly in the person of Jesus, who comes from the lineage of David (Matthew 1:6–16), and will reign forever as King of Kings and Lord of Lords (Revelation 19:16).

But why David? Why make a covenant with this violent, adulterous man, unfit to build the temple? The Scriptures tell us that David's heart was fully devoted to the Lord his God (1 Kings 11:4). His devotion had nothing to do with his strength, wealth, or power but reflected his heart of contrition and worship, born from sacred waiting.

Once again God establishes a covenant with one who had learned not to charge ahead with his own plans and desires, but to wait on the Lord. David's lifelong experience of attentiveness, willingness, and responsiveness to God—sacred waiting—turned his heart repeatedly to worship and established a worthy foundation for the covenant the Lord would make with him.

DAVID AND US

From the hills of Bethlehem to the halls of the royal palace, David knew that waiting and worship belong together. We cannot wait on God without worshiping Him, neither can we worship God without truly waiting on Him. It begs the question for each of us: How much does worship feature in our own lives?

Perhaps, like many other people, worship plays a relatively small role in our lives; in part, because we fail to wait well on the Father. We don't spend much time *with* Him or even thinking *of* Him. We don't turn our attention to Him very often throughout the day. We don't walk with Him so much as report back to Him. And consequently much of what we do in the course of a day responds to the urgent and important that others thrust upon us. Worship hardly thrives in such blinkered lives, lives grounded more in Greek thought, with humanity at the center, than Hebrew thought, centered on God.

When a waiter approaches our table, his demeanor and body language makes all the difference to our experience. We deeply appreciate those who come warmly and show interest in us, who give us their full attention because they consider us worthy of it, who demonstrate some level of respect for us. We don't ask for their worship in the sense that we might worship the Lord, but when they deem us "worth it," it certainly makes the encounter a much richer one.

Similarly, as we wait on God, worship is foundational. We can, of course, pray with relative disinterest, read His Word with boredom, sing to Him halfheartedly, or barely glance His way throughout the day. Such lack of engagement denotes lack of worship. But He *is* "worth it."

Sacred waiting must involve meaningful worship. Indeed, our lives find their greatest fulfillment and joy in worshiping the Lord—making Him the center of everything—as we wait on Him.

GROUP DISCUSSION

1. The Hebrew worldview saw everything centered on the divine reality, while the Greeks placed humanity at the center of everything. How can we better nurture a Hebrew approach to the world rather than a Greek approach?

2. What might David have learned about worship as he lived the life of a young shepherd?

3. Have you found that waiting on God in both presence and service nurtures worship in your own life?

4. Why is hope—Christian hope (confidence)—such a

foundational element for our worship? What steps might we take to focus more on God's irrevocable love for us than on God's provision for us? And what are the dangers of a hope grounded primarily in His provision?

5. What is the dominant view of worship among Christian believers, from your experience? Does this align with the biblical model of lifestyle worship? If not, how could we begin to make a better alignment?

CHAPTER 5

JESUS: WAIT AND OBEY

Jesus, teach me to walk your way, to embrace waiting, listening, and suffering as you did. Teach me obedience through the hardships and hurts of life, that I might walk closer to you and know you more fully. Amen.

The Gospels are filled with surprises. The blind and the lame are healed. The dead are raised. Demons are cast out. Wild men are restored to their right minds. Thousands of pigs hurl themselves to their death into the Sea of Galilee. The disciples act nobly sometimes and foolishly at other times. They willingly travel the countryside without much more than the shirts on their backs, asking for shelter and food as they move from town to town preaching, and then sit in a boat during a storm at sea, fearing for their lives.

But an undercurrent exists in the Gospels that might leave us puzzled. Jesus, the Son of God, the miracle worker, the authoritative Teacher, describes himself as subservient to the Father. *He waits on Him.* We don't find the word *wait* used to describe Jesus in the Gospels, but the concept pervades their pages. John's gospel, in particular, reports some extraordinary sayings of Jesus.

> Jesus gave them this answer: "I tell you the truth, *the Son can do nothing by himself; he can do only what he sees his Father doing,* because whatever the Father does the Son also does."
>
> John 5:19

The Son did *nothing* by himself. Rather, He spent His earthly ministry watching what the Father did and emulating it. It's a remarkable claim. How easily Jesus might have been moved by His own heart to reach out and touch the blind, the lame, and the demon-possessed. How easily He might have "done His own thing" and impressed the crowds. Instead, He simply looked to see what the Father was doing—and joined in. That's waiting in its richest form. And lest the disciples miss the importance of the point, Jesus reiterated it later in the same speech.

> "By myself I can do nothing; I judge only as I hear, and my judgment is just, for I seek not to please myself but him who sent me."
>
> John 5:30

At the end of Jesus' ministry, He reminds His disciples:

> "The words that I say to you I do not speak on My own initiative, but the Father abiding in Me does His works."
>
> John 14:10 NASB

"These words you hear are not my own; they belong to the Father who sent me."

John 14:24

Over and over Jesus said that He listened to the Father and spoke only what the Father spoke to Him; His life was a constant experience of the Father's Presence and a constant responsiveness to the Father's leading.

Jesus liked to use the word *abiding*. It reflected His own life of sacred waiting. He abided in the Father and the Father abided in Him. Similarly we are invited, or even called, to abide in them. This abiding means that we remain intimately connected with the Lord like the branch of a tree.

Furthermore, Jesus' words, actions, and judgments did not spring from His own intuition or wisdom. He reflected the Father's words, actions, and judgments. Even the Son found himself waiting on the Father—and doing it so perfectly that He could truly say to Philip, "Anyone who has seen me has seen the Father" (John 14:9). Sacred waiting achieved its perfect result. When we spend enough time with the Father we become increasingly like Him.

Jesus evidently waited on the Father moment by moment, always attentive to Him, even through His suffering. And His suffering bore fruit, just as it can in our lives.

WAITING AND SUFFERING

Suffering inherently involves waiting (in the common sense of the word)—waiting for relief, for comfort, for its end. If pain or grief had immediate resolution, we would not suffer. If rejection did not matter and oppression stopped in an instant, we would not suffer. If all our questions had answers and our fears vanished as quickly as they surfaced, we would not suffer. Suffering means waiting. It's that period between being wounded and healed. And to wait on the Father (in the sense of sacred waiting) during seasons of suffering may be the toughest wait of all.

The writer to the Hebrews made an extraordinary observation of Jesus in this regard.

> During the days of Jesus' life on earth, he offered up prayers and petitions with loud cries and tears to the one who could save him from death, and he was heard because of his reverent submission. *Although he was a son, he learned obedience from what he suffered* and, once made perfect, he became the source of eternal salvation for all who obey him.
>
> Hebrews 5:7–9

Jesus learned obedience from what He suffered. What does this mean? Did suffering teach Him to be obedient? Had He been *dis*obedient before the incarnation? It's inconceivable that the harmony of the Trinity was imperfect before Jesus suffered on earth; that He did not really practice submission within the Godhead until He had struggled as a man, until He had melted into "loud cries and tears" in the garden of Gethsemane.

How then shall we understand Jesus' experience?

Owen Crouch, who has meticulously diagrammed most of the sentences of the New Testament, has suggested that Jesus learned what was involved in obedience "in this kind of world."[1] It's one thing to be obedient when all is well and easy and obedience has no negative consequences. But in a fallen world—"this kind of world"—obedience to the Father can mean opposition from those around us.

On April 20, 1999, Columbine High School (Colorado)

To wait on the Father during seasons of suffering may be the toughest wait of all.

student Valeen Schnurr hid beneath a computer desk in the library as Eric Harris and Dylan Klebold stalked through the facility armed with guns, pipe bombs, and Molotov cocktails. Tragically, many students had fled to the library for safety, not realizing the killers would corner them there. At one point during the terrifying ordeal, Schnurr was down on her hands and knees bleeding, already hit by thirty-four shotgun pellets, saying, "Oh my God, Oh my God, don't let me die," when heavily armed Dylan Klebold asked her if she believed in God. She said yes; he asked why. "Because I believe, and my parents brought me up that way," she said. Klebold reloaded his weapon but didn't shoot her again, moving on with Harris to shoot others, ultimately killing twelve students and a teacher and wounding twenty-three others before the carnage stopped.[2]

In that moment, Val Schnurr, who survived the horrific massacre that day, knew that obedience to God could prove very costly. Would she deny her faith in the face of death, or remain resolute despite the danger? Obedience can exact a high price.

Jesus learned firsthand the violent consequences of obedience. But He also learned firsthand the emotional angst into which obedience sometimes plunges us. The writer to the Hebrews tells us that Jesus "offered up prayers and petitions with loud cries and tears" (5:7). The Greek word the writer uses for *cry* describes a cry "which a man does not choose to utter but it is wrung from him in the stress of some tremendous tension or searing pain."[3]

We know that cry all too well: the heartache that comes with a motionless ultrasound during a pregnancy, or a knock on the front door from military personnel. It's the grief that pours forth uncontrollably when a daughter is raped or cancer returns. It's the cry of a family devastated by alcoholism or substance abuse. With hearts ready to burst, we cannot restrain that involuntary cry.

Obedience in good times seems considerably easier than

obedience in the midst of grief. When the immediate outcome of obedience is pleasure and reward, we face a very different dynamic than when the outcome is likely suffering, loss, or death. Jesus learned obedience in an entirely new way through the suffering He endured as a man.

Renowned British Bible scholar William Barclay notes:

> The Greek phrase for "He learned from what he suffered" . . . is a thought which keeps recurring in the Greek thinkers. They were always connecting *mathein*, to learn, and *pathein*, to suffer. Aeschylus, the earliest of the Greek dramatists, had as a kind of continual text: "Learning comes from suffering." He calls suffering a kind of *savage grace* from the gods.[4]

OBEDIENCE AND GRACE

How many of us view suffering as "a savage grace"?

In *The School of Dying Graces*, former Azusa Pacific University President Richard Felix tells the moving story of his wife Vivian's epic battle with breast cancer. Vivian's first diagnosis came in February 1997, and her body succumbed to the aggressive cancer in June 1999. Their journey together over those last thirty months of Vivian's life reflected powerful doses of not only chemotherapy and radiotherapy but also faith, hope, and love. Deeply touching are the lessons of grace that came through this suffering. Felix writes of the grace of letting go, the grace of seeing with the eyes of faith, the grace of dependence, the grace of surrender, the grace of gratitude, and the grace of transformation.

> Now, four years after my wife's death, I have begun to understand [that] . . . in the way she faced adversity with faith and died with grace, she planted seeds that [are] already ripening into a great harvest.[5]

Vivian's death touched the lives of many as she learned a new obedience through what she suffered and as she waited on the Father through it all.

Sheldon Vanauken also experienced this savage grace. In his book *A Severe Mercy,*[6] he recounts the relentless way in which God used the premature death of his wife, and a friendship with C. S. Lewis, to draw him from atheism into faith. Ultimately, the tragic passing of his wife became a catalyst for his own conversion—a severe mercy.

This savage side of grace, the lessons that can only be learned by receiving grace, not dispensing it, no doubt found a deeper place in Jesus' life through His suffering and death. As He waited on the Father throughout His suffering, He also learned the grace that accompanies such obedience—"grace to help us in our time of need" (Hebrews 4:16).

In times of need we typically want salvation, and we define that as the immediate solution to our immediate need. If we're battling sickness, grace should mean healing. If we're facing bankruptcy, grace should mean money. If we're dealing with a broken marriage, grace should mean plenty of support, sympathy, and compassion from others. But the grace that Richard and Vivian Felix experienced, and the grace that Jesus himself received, looked much different. God's Presence did not reduce the pain or delay the death. Instead, grace meant the gift of growth in the inner person. It meant inner transformation. It enabled them to see something larger than the circumstances. It provided hope when despair may have overtaken them. It gave assurance in the face of apparent defeat. It made their lives more meaningful than they had ever imagined or experienced. Grace changed their perspective. Grace lifted their eyes beyond the horizon of their pain to a promise that could not be disappointed and a love that could not be diminished.

In a sense, it's a savage grace—the grace received out of pain and suffering. And while we might prefer a more comfortable path, it's this *path of pain* that potentially saves us from the shortsighted and self-centered existence for which we might otherwise settle.

Sacred waiting during seasons of suffering is the graduate school of spiritual formation. Yet the notion that God may alleviate our despair but leave us in suffering hardly appeals to us. Similarly, while we want a quick and complete escape from our own hardships, we desire the same for others. It's hard to walk the journey of suffering with other people, never truly able to explain the causes, the reasons, or the purposes; never able to fully heal the hurting hearts. We want to avoid the suffering of others as much as to escape our own. Waiting on God through *their* hardship demands courage, too.

> *It's this path of pain that potentially saves us from the shortsighted and self-centered existence for which we might otherwise settle.*

SINKING INTO HUMANITY

Well-meaning evangelists tell us that "coming to Christ" will lift us out of our predicaments, improve our circumstances, and raise us above the risks of life. "God has a great plan for your life, to prosper you." And our spiritual cataracts keep us from seeing the truth.

The life of the Kingdom is not found in mystical euphoria or heightened prosperity. To become like Christ does not mean absconding from the pain and suffering of the world, but rather entering fully into it. We want exaltation without humiliation and resurrection without death. We pray for angelic choirs, not demonic tormentors. Our hearts want to "fly away," not remain shackled to the oppression and violence of this world.

But the sons and daughters of God—those who understand

their Father's heart—continue to sink into humanity; not to be overcome by it but to minister to it.

At times we're tempted to become God's advisor, critical that He doesn't impose the equivalent of spiritual "martial law" on a world gone mad. We're confident that we know what's best, if He'd just listen to us and put some of that omnipotence to work. We assume for just a moment that He doesn't see or doesn't care.

But strangely, He calls us not to fix humanity but to sink into it.

Jesus did not sprinkle fairy dust from a crop duster to magically cure the nameless masses. Instead, He became like us, walked among us, suffered with us, and pointed the way for us. When we face heartache and hardship, we have opportunity to bear witness to our ultimate confidence in the Father.

We share in the fellowship of Christ's suffering (Philippians 3:10). We fix our eyes on the One who endured the cross and its hostility (Hebrews 12:2–3). We embrace our suffering as steps toward eternal glory (1 Peter 5:10).

None of this comes naturally or easily. In the flesh we want to avoid the corruption of humanity—the pain and sorrow, the bumps and bruises. But as we look to Jesus, He invites us not to flee but to follow. And the path leads into the tasteless darkness where we might become salt and light.

The children of God do not abandon the brokenness of the world but reach into it, to share the suffering and impart amazing grace. Our sacred waiting on the Lord does not simply catch us up into a mystical encounter with Him but sends us out into a parched world to share its thirst and bring hope.

I WANT TO KNOW

Richard Rohr, a Franciscan priest, has noted, "We love closure, resolution, and clarity, while thinking that we are people of 'faith'! How strange that the very word *faith* has come to mean its exact opposite."[7]

Will Brian return safely from Iraq? Will Mina recover from her brain aneurysm? Will fourteen-year-old Keith act on his suicidal thoughts? Will chemotherapy conquer Amy's cancer? Will my kids grow up to love Christ? Will their marriages survive? Will we be able to pay our next set of bills? Will my surgery be successful? Will my third-grader get a good teacher? Will my car last another six months? Will I be able to retire comfortably?

Each day produces multiple uncertainties. Will it be OK? We want to know.

We don't ask the Lord to reveal a twenty-year plan. "Please just give me a little certainty." Meanwhile, we rehearse all the possibilities and our responses in each scenario. If this, then that; but if something else, then what?

As people of faith, how should we live?

We spend much of our emotional energy in pursuit of answers, insights, glimpses, and clarity. We fret because of the uncertain, worry about the unforeseen, and stress over the unknown. We may agonize over the future and lose sleep over the "not yet." But Christ calls us to peace, contentment, and confidence; to faith. Such faith may not resolve all confusion but produces confidence in the midst of it. Turbulence may persist, but we trust. Pressure may rise, but we have peace. And it comes as a product of sacred waiting.

As Rohr notes, too often we view faith as our key to clarity. We believe in God; He should tell us what we want to know. We pray; He should provide. We serve; He should save.

Somewhere along the way, we have reversed the biblical definition of faith. Faith has become our means to sight. Yet the faith modeled by Jesus had little to do with an orderly, safe, sanitary, or "successful" life. He held to faith despite homelessness, harm, rejection, abandonment, and death.

We prefer the modern version of faith that entitles us to divine answers for future questions. *I want to know!* The apostle Paul also said, "I want to know." But he added to it. He wrote, "I want to know *Christ*." For Paul, that was foundational. Sacred waiting extends far beyond gathering information. It guides us into a meaningful relationship. It's not *what* we know, but *who* we know. Paul says something strange to our ears and shocking to our sensibilities:

> I want to know Christ and the power of his resurrection *and the fellowship of sharing in his sufferings, becoming like him in his death, and so, somehow, to attain to the resurrection from the dead.*
>
> Philippians 3:10–11

How many of us desire the fellowship of sharing in Christ's sufferings? We'd like to share in His power and miracles. We'd like to share in His contentment and Kingdom. We'd like to share in His love and eternal life. But His sufferings? Suffering lacks any glorious element whatsoever. It implies more judgment than blessing. It distracts our attention and limits our service. It hinders our effectiveness for the Kingdom. Why would we embrace "the fellowship of Christ's suffering"? We fervently hope that waiting on the Lord will alleviate our suffering, not perpetuate it.

Perhaps Paul meant it figuratively, as though we might know Christ and simply show gratitude for the suffering He endured on our behalf. But that's not what Paul wrote. He desired to share in the suffering, the death, and the resurrection of Jesus, knowing that as he remained obedient to Christ in hardship, he'd be shaped more profoundly to live with Christ for eternity. Instead of a better life, we're offered a better hope of intimacy with God—a relationship that carries us through and not around pain and loss.

IT HURTS

Life would be much nicer without cuts, bruises, and headaches. Broken limbs, burnt skin, aching teeth, and blistered feet don't delight any of us. There's no joy in injury. It hurts. But the physical elements of this world fail to compare with the social, emotional, or spiritual components. We experience the deepest wounds not in the flesh but in the spirit.

When our bed is awash with tears during the night, when our stomachs knot tighter and tighter, when our hearts feel ready to break with the agony of grief or conflict, what can we do? For my head, I take a capsule and expect relief within thirty minutes. But for my spirit, what fast fix exists?

The broken marriage, the drug-dazed child, and the downsized workplace break our hearts. When others criticize or reject us, what fast-acting relief can ease our pain? When we fail in a task, a ministry, or a relationship, what instant balm exists for our tenderized feelings?

In a culture that avidly avoids pain, we gravitate toward one-minute theology and microwaved spirituality.

None of us is eager to accept the assertion that "God loves you and has a difficult plan for your life." When Henri Nouwen wrote about the power of the "wounded healer," surely he didn't mean that we ought to embrace being perpetually or repeatedly wounded. Who'd sign up for that? Our woundedness surely belongs to our past, not our present.

Yet historically, suffering has nearly always been the doorway to meaningful ministry. It's the paradox of the gospel that life comes from death, purpose arises from pain, and meaning emerges from misery.

Renowned author and psychologist Larry Crabb rebuked the crass happiness syndrome of modern evangelicalism by writing: "I have no strategies in mind to give you a better marriage, better kids,

> *We gravitate toward one-minute theology and microwaved spirituality.*

a more complete recovery from sexual abuse, or quicker healing after your divorce. Nor, I believe, does God."[8] Crabb notes that the good-behavior-leads-to-blessings theology has become endemic within the church today, but this "Law of Linearity" has never held true. Instead, we need to discover the embrace of God without specific expectations as to how He should perform. If He holds us, nothing can ultimately harm us.

Crabb's conclusions don't fit the "successful" faith I want.

Can't the gospel liberate me from all my blindness, captivity, and pain? Does God not desire my immediate healing and happiness? Is there no simple formula by which I can discard my past baggage, erase my past mistakes, and quickly repair my brokenness? I can accept a cross, provided the resurrection comes quickly.

It hurts. Yes. But there's hope. St. John of the Cross, the sixteenth-century Spanish monk and mystic, described it as "the dark night of the soul." That dark night has various stages. The first stage is desolation. The last stage is consolation. In between, God holds our hand, purifies our heart, and prepares us for eternity.

The apostle John, describing Christ in the Revelation, most typically identifies Him as "the Lamb" or "the Lamb who was slain."[9] Perhaps our pain will produce a special affinity and intimacy with Him for eternity, as we cling to Him now while awash in our sorrow. Our deepest spiritual formation occurs not as we flee our distress, but as we face Him and wait on Him. We grow most when we wait.

Sacred waiting endures and obeys—remains faithful—when everything around us seems tempestuous. Sacred waiting nurtures our deepest strength, hope, and intimacy with Christ.

THE NEW COVENANT

Just as Noah, Abraham, Moses, and David had learned to wait on the Lord before He established covenants with them and their descendants, so also Jesus practiced attentiveness, willingness, and responsiveness to the Father. And we should not overlook the significance of Jesus' waiting on the Father. The unhurried but purposeful life that Jesus models for us flies in the face of the scurrying efforts of our day to achieve great things. Yet God consistently made covenants with those whose lives demonstrated consistent waiting on Him, irrespective of the circumstances or time periods involved.

We can only speculate on the circumstances of our lives today if Jesus had been in too much of a hurry or just a little too afraid to wait on the Father's timing. Yet every step He took, every word He spoke, and everything He did emerged from His constant attentiveness to the Father. And He willingly endured all manner of indignity, shame, and pain in order to establish a new covenant for all humanity through the shedding of His blood.

For those of us who think there's not a moment to lose, not a day to waste, not a week to idle away, the example of these Old Testament saints and Jesus himself confronts our delusion. Beneath our hurry—even to do the work of the Father—lie several false assumptions. First, we assume that we know *what* needs to be done to advance the Kingdom. Second, we assume that we know *when* it needs to be done (now). Third, we assume that we're the ones God chooses and needs for the tasks at hand. And finally, we assume that if we jump straight to work we'll attract His favor and blessing. But in the process, do we prayerfully listen? Have we yet learned obedience through that which *we* suffer?

In a world that hungers for achievement and glory, it's natural to assume that these same core values also apply to the Kingdom of God. But Jesus shows us another way: not the priority of sensational service, but sensitive surrender. And as we practice this most basic aspect of sacred waiting, remaining obedient and faithful, we discover a life in step with His Spirit.

JESUS AND US

The writer to the Hebrews reminded his readers to look to Jesus, especially to find the strength to endure hardship. He exhorted them and us with these words:

> Let us fix our eyes on Jesus, the author and perfecter of our faith, who for the joy set before him endured the cross, scorning its shame, and sat down at the right hand of the throne of God. Consider him who endured such opposition from sinful men, so that you will not grow weary and lose heart.
>
> Hebrews 12:2–3

Waiting on the Father does not guarantee ease and comfort. Just the opposite: it softens our hearts to suffer as never before. As Jesus wept over Jerusalem, so we might find ourselves weeping over the corruption and destiny of a world far from God.

One important question remains, however. Will suffering—ours and that of others—teach us deeper levels of trust and obedience, or turn us against the Son who has experienced death itself for us? If waiting on the Father means hardship while we attend to Him and rejection if we serve Him, will we have the courage to carry the cross?

Such waiting on the Lord serves as a crucible in our own lives: teaching us, refining us, and commissioning us to levels of obedience and ministry we have never before considered. May such waiting be increasingly true for us.

GROUP DISCUSSION

1. What would it take for you to be able to say, like Jesus, "I do not speak on my own initiative"? In other words, how do you so walk by the Spirit that your life becomes more genuinely godly?

2. Describe a season of suffering you have endured (perhaps sickness, death, or even sleepless nights over a child's health). How did you respond during that suffering? What did you learn from it then, or what might you learn from it now as you reflect on it?

3. How do you feel about the idea of "savage grace"—that is, the grace that comes through very hard experiences? Is this something to resent or receive?

4. Do you find the idea of "sinking into humanity" (delivering grace to others during their suffering—and perhaps during our own) appealing or repelling? Discuss this idea.

5, How does "setting your eyes on Jesus" enable you to practice sacred waiting—and obedience—during seasons of suffering?

TRANSITION

Thus far I've defined sacred waiting with two key words—*presence* and *service*—and drawn on the analogy of a table waiter whose first priority is to be "present" for the customers, making them feel comfortable, not rushing them, but ready to take their order when they are ready. But this presence has another aspect to it.

Colin and Kristy are friends of ours who love to eat at Outback Steakhouse. In fact, they have visited the local Outback so many times that they have gotten to know the waiters there very well. Over the years they've even had a couple of them to their home for dinner! More important, the waiters have also gotten to know them. By spending increasing time waiting on them, the waiters have learned their preferences and favorite items. In fact, the relationship has gotten so close over time that when Colin admired a shirt a waiter wore one night, the manager came out and presented a similar shirt to Colin on his next visit!

Waiting on the Lord has much the same impact. It's not simply that we stand ready to serve, but that the more time we spend in His Presence the better we get to know Him and, naturally, some of what He would like even before He speaks. This is waiting with meaning and purpose. It's the kind of waiting based on relationship, not a menu.

The theme of sacred waiting appears not only in the lives of the major biblical figures that we've considered. It also appears as a foundational element within each of the major liturgical seasons on the church calendar.

For at least seventeen hundred years, the church has divided each year into a series of major seasons—Advent, Lent, Easter, and Pentecost—based on the major events in the life and ministry of Jesus. *Advent*: the coming of Christ. *Lent*: the wilderness testing and the temptation of Christ. *Easter*: the death, burial, and resurrection of Christ. *Pentecost*: the coming of the Holy Spirit as promised by Christ. Each of these seasons is immersed in sacred waiting, as we'll see, and has the potential to guide us to deeper confidence in Christ and a richer walk with Him.

Many believers are relatively oblivious to the church calendar, because many congregations make little mention of them. Other than Christmas Day and Easter Sunday, both of which our culture helps us recall, the liturgical calendar has suffered serious neglect in many quarters of the church—neglect of use, neglect of significance, or both.

Interestingly, many churches are now starting to rediscover the value of the liturgical calendar to help us establish annual rhythms for our spiritual lives. Consequently, in the next few chapters we'll explore how these biblical seasons might continue to expand our understanding and experience of waiting on God.

CHAPTER 6

THE ADVENT WAIT

O God, you who came in light and glory, in meekness and humility; in my despair and in my joy, come again now. Come with compassion and mercy. Come with grace and forgiveness. Come with love and comfort. And I come to you. Amen.

Charles Dickens' classic portrayal of the old and miserly Ebenezer Scrooge in his 1843 novel *A Christmas Carol* captured the heart and imagination of Victorian England. Scrooge had devoted his life to accumulating wealth and displayed open contempt for everything but money. When the Christmas season arrived, he dismissed all hospitable invitations with his infamous "Bah! Humbug!" and declared Christmas a fraud. To his mind, it served no useful purpose at all.

Dickens used the story to attack various social ills of his time, including the indifference of the wealthy to the poor, whom they described at times as "surplus population."[1] But just as important, the plot also reveals the redemptive possibility for everyone, as Scrooge's own hard heart is transformed by the terror of his ghostly visions one night. Christmas, therefore, signified both a season of hope and a season of transformation. Indeed, the turnaround in Scrooge validated the anticipation that people associated with Christmas Day.

Historically, Advent—the four Sundays before Christmas, on the church calendar since the fourth century—expresses a period of growing anticipation. The first two Sundays represent a period of repentance, as followers of Jesus acknowledge the darkness in and around them and their desperate need for a Savior. The third Sunday reflects a Sunday of promise and rising hope that the Savior draws near. Finally, the fourth Sunday bursts forth with anticipation. Messiah's birth and coming are at hand. Thus Advent denotes a season of increased attention to Christ—acknowledgment of our sin and waywardness, an appeal for absolution and deliverance, and anticipation that the Deliverer is about to arrive. This is sacred waiting.

ADVENT

Advent provides an opportunity for us to pause, reflect, and wait on God—the One who comes to us in the flesh—in fresh ways.

For most of us, the Christmas season usually denotes the busiest and most chaotic time of the year. With just a month between Thanksgiving and Christmas Day, there's no time for quiet reflection or downtime. From Black Friday (the crazy bargain-hunting that begins the day after Thanksgiving) until Christmas Eve, we plan, search, buy, cook, wrap, and hurry. The goal for many of us is simply survival, not attending humbly to the Lord.

There is so much to do! Light displays to put up, trees to trim; Christmas pageants to schedule or attend; parties to host or participate in; Christmas brunch or dinner to prepare. There are mail orders to place; shopping and waiting in long checkout lines; gifts to wrap, cards to write. The rush, congestion, and distraction of the season can be overwhelming for most of us.

The biblical story of Advent—that period immediately before the arrival of the Christ—calls us to wait on God in deeper ways, even while the time flies by. Thus it becomes not only a story to tell but a life to embrace.

A CAST OF WAITERS

All the key figures who appear in the first few pages of Luke's gospel demonstrate a keen attentiveness and responsiveness to God: Elizabeth and Zechariah, Mary and Joseph, Simeon and Anna. When we read their stories, we quickly realize that they represent well-seasoned waiters.

Elizabeth and Zechariah, described as "upright in the sight of God, observing all the Lord's commandments and regulations blamelessly" (Luke 1:6), had wanted a child all their lives. As with so many figures in the Old Testament, the Bible simply notes that "Elizabeth was barren." Those three words hardly capture the many seasons of hope followed by heartache, the yearning and the disappointment, the anticipation and the devastation. *Barren.* It's another word for someone who has suffered one shattered dream after another and either lost hope or given it up. But then, by divine blessing, Elizabeth becomes pregnant and secludes herself in glorious anticipation of the birth of her prophet son, John. Perhaps she felt some anxiety. For an older woman to go full-term without complications is not easy.

Zechariah shared the anticipation. The angel Gabriel had announced to him that he and Elizabeth would have a son (Luke 1:13–17). At last! But in a moment of doubt, Zechariah sought a sign, and the angelic messenger struck him dumb. He could not and would not speak until after the birth of the boy (Luke 1:18–20). For nine months, Zechariah shared the excitement of the pregnancy in silence, unable to chatter about this spectacular news.

It is important to note that the angel Gabriel spoke to Zechariah as he waited on the Lord. Scripture tells us that Zechariah "was performing his priestly service before God" (Luke 1:8 NASB), and had entered the temple of the Lord to burn incense, while a multitude of people stood outside and prayed. The circumstances are significant. Zechariah had given his full attention to the Lord— literally waiting at His table—when the angel appeared and declared the news. The temple was a sacred place and perfect for sacred waiting. Little wonder then that it plays a role in the birth stories of John the Baptist and Jesus.

Meanwhile, far to the north, Mary and Joseph had their married lives ahead of them. As an engaged couple, they anticipated marriage, intimacy, children, and family life. But an angel of the Lord came to Mary before her wedding day, and said, "Do not be afraid, Mary, you have found favor with God. You will be with child and give birth to a son, and you are to give him the name Jesus" (Luke 1:30–31). *Don't be afraid?* This could mess up everything! Yet Mary submits to the Lord and bravely replies, "I am the Lord's servant. . . . May it be to me as you have said" (Luke 1:38).

Mary's response to the angel demonstrates a heart accustomed to waiting on the Lord. She listened well and then presented herself in humble service to the will of the Lord, even though the request could entail great personal cost.

The pregnancy could end her engagement to Joseph. Once her pregnancy started to show, it would certainly shame her in the eyes of the people who knew her. Perhaps she experienced nights of fear. What might a God-conceived child look like? Who would care for her as a single mom if Joseph broke off the engagement? But those who wait on the Lord know that faith, not fear, must prevail. We can trust Him even when everything we have wanted and dreamed about seems at risk.

Not long after the birth of Christ, Simeon, an old man living in Jerusalem, saw the newborn Jesus. Luke tells us that Simeon was "righteous and devout. He was *waiting* for the consolation of Israel, and the Holy Spirit was upon him. It had been revealed to him by the Holy Spirit that he would not die before he had seen the Lord's Christ" (Luke 2:25–26). Once again the temple comes into the story. Simeon "came in the Spirit into the temple" (Luke 2:27 NASB) and then saw the child Jesus.

The phrase "came in the Spirit" might have various interpretations, but at the very least it suggests that Simeon's spiritual antennae were on high alert. He came to the temple for one purpose: to honor God and to worship Him, deeply sensitive to the Presence of the Lord. And there in the Presence of God, and with an open heart, Simeon unexpectedly found himself in the Presence of the Messiah. Waiting on God produced an extraordinary encounter with God, albeit with a certain bittersweetness. On the one hand, the great joy of seeing the Messiah. On the other hand, knowing that once he had seen Him, he would die. But Simeon saw only the privilege. Waiting on God never evoked dread. Indeed, when the baby Jesus was placed in his arms, he blessed God, and said, "Sovereign Lord, as you have promised, you now dismiss your servant in peace. For my eyes have seen your salvation" (Luke 2:29–30). Simeon's longing was fulfilled. He was at peace.

Similarly, Scripture tells us the story of Anna, an eighty-four-year-old widow, who never left the temple, fasting and praying both day and night. Why? Because she was among the many who "were looking forward to the redemption of Jerusalem" (Luke 2:38). Oppressed by the Roman occupation, she and many others longed for the day when Messiah would come and deliver Israel from bondage. And Anna's anticipation of Messiah was not an occasional afterthought. It preoccupied her waking life. She waited on God with prayer and fasting and with great persistence. Widowed after just seven years of marriage, she had not left the temple in nearly sixty years! (Luke

2:36–37). And then, at the very moment that Simeon delivered his prophetic word upon seeing Jesus, she also arrived on the scene and recognized the One whom she had longed to see for six decades.

The coming of Christ—His advent—involved all manner of waiting on God. A barren wife, a young maiden, a dying man, and an old widow all model hearts yielded to God, alert to His Presence, and diligent in His service. Their stories, their experiences, and their examples turn Advent into a season of powerful teaching on sacred waiting.

Ralph Waldo Emerson once said, "How much of human life is lost in waiting?" The typical Christmas can produce the usual waiting as people count down the days and rush to squeeze in as much as possible. And such waiting does indeed fritter away human life. But the season of Advent reminds us that human life finds its greatest meaning and blessing in sacred waiting. *Sacred waiting* actually forms the centerpiece of the biblical Christmas story.

As we learn to practice faith, hope, attentiveness, submission, and patience, we see the Child. Jesus does not yell over the blare of Christmas music. Nor does He create a spectacle more dazzling than decorations or parades. He does not force His way into our gift-opening traditions, or override our feasting and football. He tarries in the stillness.

We don't lose life when we wait on God, we find it.

Emerson's quote lacks accuracy. We don't lose life when we wait on God, we find it. Our lives will never look the same again, and they'll never have looked so good.

READY

Very few of us find ourselves ready for Christmas when it arrives each year. Take all of the decorations, gifts, cards, food, and travel plans, and add in our regular routine of home and work, and Martha Stewart could hardly pull it off without a few moments of insanity. It's hard to feel ready. On the other hand, for others of us "ready" is not possible. We dread the holidays, filled as they may be with painful memories or experiences of loneliness. We're ready to get *past* Christmas!

As moms and dads, we may be counting down for school to finish, for a few days to sleep in, and maybe some time off work. In that case, we may have been ready for a month!

Churches that recognize Advent sometimes use a specific set of Bible readings associated with the season. Those readings include the words of John the Baptist, who came as a voice crying in the wilderness: "Make ready the way of the Lord" (Matthew 3:3 NASB). Advent and Christmas call each of us primarily to a readiness for Christ. Yet we frequently stand ill-prepared for Him. Perhaps being ready for Christ is toughest of all. Why?

Some of us struggle to wait on Christ because He has high expectations. He no longer needs the gold, frankincense, and myrrh of the magi. "What gift will we give Him?" might be better rephrased "What gift would He want from us?" And it turns out He wants not our wealth but our hearts. Are we ready to yield our hearts fully to Him in love and obedience?

But to make ready the way of the Lord is also to clear everything else out of the way. Our culture has so cluttered the highway with flashing Santa signs, glittering gifts, bouncy jingles, and oversized decorations that we can barely see a way through. Can we truly look beyond the distracting sights and blaring sounds of secularism?

"Are you ready for Christmas?"

Our ultimate readiness, surprisingly, is not measured by budgets, miles, pounds, or postage stamps, but by the countercultural call to quiet and attentiveness. The ancient prophet continues to cry out and challenge us to prepare for what matters most. "Make ready the way of the Lord." But to do so—to wait on the Lord properly—may mean we'll have to slow down.

STOP THE HURRY

I live in a hurry. People don't walk quickly enough for me. Goals take too long to reach. Programs feel bogged down by minutia. Email replies are too slow. Meaningful relationships take forever to develop. And so it goes.

If I could just release the brakes, the world would function so much more efficiently and effectively. We could achieve so much more. The slowness around me breeds increasing frustration, especially my own slowness to learn, grow, change, or achieve.

Hurry up, please!

My impatience, however, reflects how unaware I am of God's work in the world. I'm waiting more on myself than on Him. I have an agenda most of the time, and His timetable rarely matches mine. We seem to be on different wavelengths. But God countermands our "Hurry up!" with His own "Listen up!" And He reminds us again, through Advent, that we usually overestimate what we can do in the short term and underestimate what He can accomplish in the long term. And His long term is the longest perspective of all. Indeed, the Lord's timetable is just that—*His* timetable, not ours.

If I had been sent to save the world, I surely would have "landed" ready to go. Arrive and conquer quickly. Every minute counts! Waste no time! But Advent challenges this haste. It reminds us that Jesus arrived as a baby, to grow, to learn, and to share life before beginning His earthly ministry.

Many of us may feel more affinity with "Hurry Christmas" than "Merry Christmas." But perhaps tucked in this story of the babe of Bethlehem is the invitation to once again discover the Lord's timing rather than our own—in all of life.

The spiritual exercise of *hush* should replace our cultural

> *Despite our self-importance and sense of urgency, Christ sets the pace and determines the results that matter most.*

inclination to rush. Despite our self-importance and sense of urgency, Christ sets the pace and determines the results that matter most. And often, while we celebrate His coming to us, we ought to reaffirm our coming to Him—in humility, in contentment, in surrender, in readiness, and in worship, much as the magi of the East modeled.

HIS COMING, OUR COMING

In August 2007, my friend Joe and his wife took a week's vacation together. Joe served as a church pastor, and they needed a break. The week away rejuvenated their spirits and replenished some of their energy. They talked about the future and made plans together. Already they'd been married for over twenty years.

But the following week, Joe's wife dropped her bombshell. She wanted a divorce. In fact, she and a client had conducted an affair for months.

Joe felt shattered. He needed to move out of the house immediately but had nowhere to go. Dazed and shell-shocked, he decided to borrow a car and drive immediately to Idaho, where his aging parents lived. For twenty years—most of his married life—he'd had minimal contact with them. In his own words, he had hurt them greatly. But what else could he do in this crisis? Where else could he go where he could buy some time to clarify his thinking and plan his next steps?

The drive to the old family homestead overlooking the Idaho Valley took many hours. The roads seemed irritatingly congested, and roadwork slowed the trip even more. It was late in the evening—about 11:00—as Joe approached the family's ten-acre property that had birthed fond memories for three generations.

He pulled over on the shoulder of the road, uncertain whether or not he could actually face his mom and dad, overwhelmed with this pain and burden. He considered heading to a local hotel for the night. Yes, that would be best; then call them in the morning and drive out to see them.

But a voice within urged him, "Go on home." Reluctantly, Joe slipped the car back into drive and eased back onto the road for the final five miles of the journey.

As he approached the family home, he saw a strange glow. It was mid-August and the night still had plenty of heat in it. But this late at night, what could produce such a glow? Then he saw it.

His parents had hired someone to put up all their Christmas lights. Lights bedecked the house and the driveway. Decorations stood out on the front lawn. And Joe's parents—in their eighties—were sitting quietly on the front porch, where they had maintained a loving vigil for many hours looking down the road for his arrival.

Their grace triumphed over his shame. Their love dispelled his anxiety.

As Joe told me his story, tears filled his eyes. In the midst of his pain and confusion, his parents reflected Christ to him. Their home became a sanctuary for him a week each month over the following six months as he processed his brokenness. That godly older couple became a source of grace and healing for Joe's woundedness.

How appropriate that they should put out the Christmas lights! Those lights, reserved for Advent each year, signaled not only the coming of the Son of God (the Light of the world), but that August, they signaled the coming of their own son.

How appropriate that during Advent we bedeck our homes with lights. More than just pretty decorations, they serve as important symbols. They affirm our commitment to be light in the darkness. And they remind us that the Father sits on the front porch for *our* coming—the other advent.

ALFRED DELP

Many Christians recognize Dietrich Bonhoeffer, the German Lutheran pastor who was arrested by the Nazis for plotting against Hitler and who was eventually hanged on April 9, 1945, at thirty-nine years of age, just three weeks before the fall of Berlin. Less well-known is Alfred Delp.

Born a year after Bonhoeffer, Delp served the German people as a Jesuit priest, staunchly committed to the way of Jesus. A week after the infamous July 20, 1944, failed attempt to assassinate Hitler, the Nazis arrested Delp, suspecting him of complicity in the plot. Over the following months he endured interrogation and torture. In January 1945, he stood trial and was found guilty, then sentenced to death. The hangman executed him on February 2, 1945—two months before Bonhoeffer's execution.

During the war and during his imprisonment in Tegel Prison, Alfred Delp reflected often on the advent. He understood the significance of waiting on God amidst the chaos of a world at war. He recognized that advent meant the freedom of God to come when and how He chooses—perhaps as a thundering warrior or as a helpless babe; perhaps at the beginning of oppression or in its advanced stages. He *is* coming—always coming—on His own terms and timetable. Meanwhile, we serve as lights in the darkness.

Throughout his life, Alfred Delp practiced the longstanding church tradition of the Advent candles. Four candles are lit during Advent—usually three purple and one rose. For each of the four Sundays of Advent, a candle is lit; all four burn brightly on the Sunday before Christmas. The white "Christ candle" is added on Christmas Day in the center of the other four. The candles lit over the four-week period symbolize the darkness of fear and hopelessness being replaced by hope. The flame of each new candle adds to the brightness, until Christ takes center stage, and we celebrate His coming again.

In some notes smuggled out of Tegel Prison, in December

1944, Delp wrote: "Light the candles wherever you can, you who have them. They are a real symbol of what must happen in Advent, what Advent must be, if we want to live."[2]

Several years earlier, Delp had spoken in detail about Advent candles as a powerful symbol of the Christian journey.

> This is a peaceful, reticent, but constant shining. This is giving light at the cost of one's own substance, so that one is consumed in the process. Anyone who wants to comprehend Christ's message of light . . . must comprehend this one thing: the mission, the duty to shine, to draw others, to seek, to heal, to do good at the cost of one's own substance.[3]

This symbolism speaks powerfully to us when we realize that our waiting at Advent—our sacred waiting—is not just anticipation of the coming of Christ, but a commitment to be consumed in His service. Just as Advent begins the Christian liturgical year, so "to do good at the cost of [our] own substance" marks the beginning of the Christian journey into a deeper place with Christ. Waiting on Him is not a wallowing in the darkness, but a shining in it. And as we give ourselves to a "peaceful, reticent, but constant shining," we find ourselves consumed. Our own ambition, our selfishness, our grasping nature, and our pride are gently burned up, but not by accident. It stems from our decision to give our all to Christ, with Christ, and for Christ; yes, to wait on Him.

Waiting on Him is not a wallowing in the darkness, but a shining in it.

"Whoever loses his life for my sake will find it" (Matthew 10:39).

The true advent, the coming of Christ, delivers us from the

frenzied pressures of materialism that increasingly dominate the end of each year. It invites us into a sacred waiting on God rather than a secular attention to gift-wrapped packages. It beckons us to an acknowledgment of the darkness and an anticipation of the Light, and then to be candles of the Kingdom in the kingdom of this world.

GROUP DISCUSSION

1. Consider the traditional Advent, which first highlights the darkness in the world around us and then progressively anticipates the Deliverer. Have you seen Advent/Christmas in this light before? How does it shape your idea of sacred waiting?

2. What comes to mind when you read about the sacred waiting modeled by all of the biblical characters associated with the coming of Christ?

3. Waiting on God meant significant personal cost for Mary and Joseph. How ready are you to say, "I am the Lord's servant. May it be to me as you have said"?

4. The Christmas lights in Joe's story represented Joe's coming home. When was the last time you truly "came home"? How can Advent become a "homecoming" for you each year?

5. The Christmas candle gives light at the cost of its own substance. What might this analogy mean for you? And how does it speak to waiting on God?

CHAPTER 7

THE LENTEN WAIT

God who provides, grant me the grace of fasting that you might gain all of me. Enable me to deny myself for your sake. Amen.

The idea seemed noble. As a young college student preparing for church ministry and already serving an internship in a large Southern California congregation, a "retreat day" sounded perfect. In the hustle of life and the crazy schedule of flitting between appointments, classes, assignments, meetings, and friends, a day away when I would specifically wait on God and give Him my full attention could only enhance the godly aura I desired as a twenty-two-year-old. And I decided to fast for the day—at least, skip lunch—to let the Lord know I meant business.

At the time, filled with enthusiasm but woefully short on either guidance or experience, I tossed my Bible in the car, grabbed a bottle of water, and hit the freeway out of the city. The trip up into the San Bernardino mountain range only took seventy-five minutes. In no time, I found myself breaking through the thick smog layer that used to blanket the Southern California basin in those days and popping out into brilliant sunshine and blue skies.

With no particular destination in mind—just "the mountains"—I finally pulled over on the side of the road where some huge boulders perched just up the hillside. That would be my place to wait on God, my spot for silence and solitude, for fasting and listening. I locked the car, clambered up the slope, and sat on the largest rock I could find.

In the next hour I heard little more than the rumbling of my own stomach. I pulled out my Bible and flipped it open randomly. The words of Scripture fell off me like beads of water off a well-waxed car. Nothing penetrated. Nothing happened. My fast, designed to make God speak so I could do my job better, turned into an abject failure. Within four or five hours I was back home, discouraged by God's failure to show up and my inability to settle down.

Many of us have experienced similar disappointments. We've switched gears amidst the chaos of our lives, paused ever so briefly, and expected the Lord to speak. We've done little or nothing to learn to wait on Him. Instead, we squeeze in a "special opportunity" for Him between all our other life engagements. Perhaps that's why historically the church has set aside an extended season of the year to fast, to create a unique space to enter His Presence more frequently and with more intentionality. We call it Lent.

LENT FOR TODAY

When Advent and Christmas finish, the next major event on the church calendar is Lent. Typically associated with the Roman Catholic Church, Orthodox churches, or a few mainline Protestant denominations, Lent has enjoyed a renewal of interest among evangelicals and independent congregations since the 1990s.

Lent (literally, "spring") dates back perhaps as far as AD 325. The season begins with Ash Wednesday and symbolically reenacts the forty days of fasting that Christ endured before His ministry was launched.[1] It builds in an annual reminder of the excesses in our own lives that may hinder us from a deeper walk with God. Our own fasting ("I gave it up for Lent") ideally heightens our sensitivity to the Presence of God and helps us identify with the experience of Jesus. The Western church tradition recognizes Sundays as "resurrection days," and exempt from the fast, which is why the period actually extends forty-*six* days until Easter Sunday.

Lent builds in an annual reminder of the excesses in our own lives that may hinder us from a deeper walk with God.

For nearly seventeen hundred years, believers have observed this fasting period. Why?

For some people it is simply tradition. They grew up keeping Lent, and still do. Their family or Christian community expected them to participate whether or not it had any particular significance to them. This produced a certain pressure to conform. If everyone else was observing Lent, so should they. But little is gained by rote observances.

The Lord once said of Israel: "This people draw near with their words and honor Me with their lip service, but they remove their hearts far from Me, and their reverence for Me consists of tradition learned by rote" (Isaiah 29:13 NASB).

Lent ought not to become a "tradition learned by rote," though it can easily slip into that rut for any of us. Instead, it gives us a fresh opportunity for a spring cleaning of the soul. It provides an occasion for us to practice heightened awareness of the Father.

Sin clogs our spiritual arteries. Comfort and materialism steadily dull our spiritual senses. The lifestyle of instant gratification deadens our spiritual sensitivity. But Lent provides a tonic for each of these afflictions.

We resolve not simply to abstain from something (chocolate, sweets, meat, dairy, eggs, television, whatever), but to use this fast as a trigger to deal with deeper issues. Just when we think we'll die if we can't get that diet soda *into* us, we realize that we are spiritually dying because we haven't worked to get other things *out* of us.

We fast to confront our corruption and discover Him in deeper ways.

We don't fast to impress God. We fast to confront our corruption and discover Him in deeper ways. Our fasting reflects a strategic, sacred wait.

There's nothing magical about forty days. Biblically, as we've seen earlier, the number represents a season of testing, but the Lord doesn't dock points for late starters or non-finishers. After the excesses of Christmas and the New Year, Lent offers valuable purging and transforming possibilities as we reenact Jesus' forty-day fast.

THE WILDERNESS AND SOLITUDE

We know very little about what happened when Jesus fasted in the wilderness. Among the gospel writers, Matthew and Luke give us the most detailed accounts (Matthew 4:1–11; Luke 4:1–13), though most of those verses deal with Satan's temptation of Jesus, which happened "*after* He had fasted forty days and forty nights" (Matthew 4:2 NASB). Mark provides the shortest account of the wilderness experience. He writes, "At once the Spirit sent him out into the desert, and he was in the desert forty days, being tempted by Satan. He was with the wild animals, and angels attended him" (Mark 1:12–13). John doesn't mention the wilderness experience at all.

Nevertheless, this wilderness fast has served throughout church history as a model for spiritual formation and a foundation for sacred waiting. To some extent, sacred waiting means clearing the decks of all else.

The Desert Fathers lived in the Egyptian desert during the fourth and fifth centuries. Violent opposition to Christianity had eased and widespread martyrdom no longer threatened Christians, but the world continued to prefer the darkness to the light (John 3:19). Consequently, various men and women decided to seek the solitude and shaping power of the wilderness rather than conform to the culture of their day. And in their isolation, they often received a steady stream of visitors who came seeking words of advice and wisdom.

One of the Desert Fathers, Arsenius—a well-educated Roman of senatorial rank—sailed secretly from Rome to Alexandria and then withdrew to a solitary life in the wilderness. He prayed, "Lord, lead me in the way of salvation," and a voice replied, "Arsenius, flee, be silent, pray always, for these are the sources of sinlessness."[2] Henri Nouwen suggests that these three phrases—*flee, be silent,* and *pray always*—summarize the spirituality of the desert. "They indicate the three ways of preventing the world from shaping us in its image and are thus the three ways to life in the Spirit."[3]

Solitude—the result of fleeing—has always provided an important context for spiritual formation. Indeed, until we establish some distance between ourselves and society, we generally live as coconspirators with our culture. We have so many things to do—places to go, and words to speak—that we seldom experience the wilderness solitude familiar to Abraham, Moses, David, and Jesus. Each of them discovered that the wilderness was far more than a place for quiet retreat where they might enjoy some privacy and perhaps recharge their batteries. It turned out to be a furnace for transformation. The wilderness, where men and women learned to wait on God in deep ways, became the seminary of the prophets.

When we feel weary, we might daydream of a place where we can sit quietly and alone for a while; a place to recover from our exhaustion. But biblically speaking, solitude meant the possibility of profound inner change. The early Desert Fathers certainly understood this, yet they refused to compromise. In the nothingness of the desert, they steadfastly confronted their own nothingness— and discovered the all-sufficiency of Christ. Their sacred waiting on Christ was not some form of passive escapism but a purposeful encounter with God and themselves.

How does this relate to the Lenten season?

At the heart of Lent lies a wilderness experience. In reenacting the solitude of Jesus by fasting in a particular way, we not only affirm the importance of refraining from our usual indulgences but we also invite the wilderness into our own spiritual journey. Have you ever done so?

In the wilderness we face our inner demons, the voices that surface more loudly than ever and seek to distract us from the Father. If you've ever fasted during Lent, you know the sudden surge in distractions or descent into apathy, which affirms the importance of the fasting. In reality, the struggle to give up something significant for Lent is the struggle to die to our false self. The comfortable, culturally acclimated, secular, false self usually sits quietly, until we decide to starve it of the noise, distractions, and self-indulgences that it thrives on. Then the battle gets serious, and we learn very quickly that our corrupt hearts do not approve of sacred waiting.

Solitude is thus the place of purification and transformation, the place of the great struggle and the great encounter. Solitude is not simply a means to an end. Solitude is its own end. It is the place where Christ remodels us in his own image and frees us from the victimizing compulsions of the world. Solitude is the place of our salvation.[4]

The church builds Lent into its annual calendar as a regular reminder that wilderness solitude and sacred waiting are foundational to our ministry and service. Even the prophets of ancient Israel frequently found fresh intensity and clarity from such seasons of wilderness solitude and waiting on God, and their messages then pierced the consciences of their hearers with divine power.

Sacred waiting demands some measure of emptying.

The lesson for many of us is that sacred waiting demands some measure of emptying—shaking off the usual routines, patterns, and distractions so that we might grow more focused and attentive and thereafter also prove more useful in His service. What kind of solitude or emptying have you built into your spiritual journey on a consistent basis?

Lent being a spring event in the Northern Hemisphere also evokes other images important to sacred waiting.

SPRING CLEANING

Most of us have lives as cluttered and unkempt as the garage or attic. Stuff everywhere. Dust bunnies. Cobwebs. We don't remember what we have, so we keep buying more. Unsorted piles of this, that, and just about everything else. Yes, the garage (or workshop) provides an uncomfortable metaphor for our lives.

Every now and then we have a spring cleaning. Out come

the dustpan and broom and, on inspired occasions, the vacuum cleaner. We may even wipe off the scummy film that builds up on the windows, and then marvel at the fresh view.

But with time and neglect, the natural order returns, which is to say no order at all.

Lent initiates a spring cleaning for the soul each year. It's a time for us to sort, sift, clean, and toss. It's an opportunity for us to admit that it is really not well with our souls—at least not as well as we'd like. It's a season for simplifying.

Most of us have little concept of moderation. We overwork, overeat, overcommit, and overspend. We insist that this is just modern life, hoping that our souls will one day agree and be at peace. We can't imagine coping or surviving without cable television, computers, and cell phones. We keep buying toys, getting gadgets, and shopping sales, hoping for happiness. We tell ourselves that "upgrades" will improve our lives. They don't.

We may have fleeting moments when this tail-chase strikes us as futile, usually prompted by exhaustion, sickness, or conflict. And we resolve that this madness must stop, which it does, until we feel better. How ironic that "feeling better" usually catapults us back onto the old path of self-destruction, the slow and unacknowledged death.

Lent provides a regular annual schedule each year to attend to the heart. It's long. Couldn't we just have a "spiritual spring cleaning weekend"? There's too much going on over a month and a half to keep focused on Lent. Ideally, we could squeeze it in between other demands. But our spiritual clutter and junk has usually spilled from the garage into the house, and in short bursts all we can do is dust and rearrange. Lent is for methodically bagging stuff and tossing it in the trash—the broken, unsafe, and unused.

Fasting throughout Lent serves multiple purposes. As we've already seen, the discipline creates a space for us to be attentive to God. It also confronts our never-say-no-to-ourselves lives. And it challenges us to reassess and reorder our spiritual priorities. Furthermore, Lent provides an opportunity to clean the windows—the windows to our souls. Regrettably, many of our windows are covered with grime. Perhaps this is a good time to break out the Windex, paper towels, gloves, and garbage bags. If we take it seriously (and prayerfully), the whole house may begin to shine by Easter.

THE WEST AUSTRALIAN WHEATBELT

My second serious foray into silence, solitude, and fasting, after the debacle in the Southern California mountains, happened in Western Australia. About six years had passed, and I decided to give it another shot. This time I planned to stay in a small hotel that a young married couple were converting into a retreat center out in the middle of the wheatbelt and a long way from anywhere. I fasted and waited on the Lord again—with dramatically different results.

It was not Lent, but I was seriously attentive to Christ. And while the setting was not the desert, the vast fields of farmland provided a relatively distraction-free environment. This time, instead of praying quickly on the side of the road and expecting a voice from heaven to inspire me, I chose to simply read Scripture and let the Word of Christ dwell in me as richly as possible.

I arrived in the late morning—a Tuesday, as I recall—and found a quiet spot in the vacant fireplace room, sat down, and started reading Scripture. I had resolved not to expect the Lord to say anything at all until I had prepared my heart to genuinely hear Him. I fasted through lunch and found some momentum building, not so much an act of my own will, but more an act of divine grace upon me. At midnight, still reading avidly and more enlivened than I ever remember being, I retired for the night.

First thing next morning, I picked up where I left off and read more. I read until about 10:30 AM, then decided to finally open my journal and write whatever the Lord laid on my heart. I was determined not to require anything of Him, but now I felt as attuned to Him as I could imagine. If He had something to say, I felt as ready as ever to hear it. And He had a simple message:

"Get in the car. Go home. And confess your sin to Kim." It was that abrupt. I knew in my spirit what He meant. But it was the last thing I expected to hear Him say. I was ready for divine revelation, for ecstatic visions, or perhaps just modest affirmation. Instead, the Lord quickened my heart to see a particular pain I had caused my wife, Kim, for a long time.

Nevertheless, I waited. Surely there'd be more. "OK, Lord, I've got that. Now, what else?" There had to be more. As focused as I'd become, as spiritually enlivened as I felt, I expected a lengthy and perhaps special treatise of some sort. I had multiple pages of blank paper to write as endlessly as I needed to. But nothing else came. Instead, I received an overpowering sense that this was a pivotal moment of obedience. Would I act as obediently as Noah, Abraham, Moses, and Jesus? I felt somewhat stunned. Nothing else? I waited for more, but nothing more came. And I knew that if I failed to obey the prompting of His Spirit on this occasion, I could not dare ask Him to speak to me again.

So I packed, drove the hour and a half back home, and poured out my heart to Kim. And that day became a day of liberation for me—not at all what I had expected two days earlier, but exactly what the Lord had planned.

Lent, the annual foray into fasting and attentiveness—into sacred waiting—provides an annual opportunity for liberation for those of us courageous enough to listen and respond. But it also draws us together as a community to hear and see God at work among us.

HUNGRY FOR GOD

Lent represents a season for us to fast collectively, not in a competitive spirit (who can give up the most or suffer the most?) but in a communal spirit (what might God be saying to us together?). As such, it is not primarily a tradition but an opportunity.

Let's be clear: The spiritual disciplines (and fasting is one of them) do not earn reward points with the Father. He does not love us more nor love us less based on our participation in the disciplines. The disciplines do not guarantee our godliness, nor do they oblige the Father to bless us with ecstatic visions or blessed insights.

Any decision to fast, be it from various foods, drink, television programs, movies, Internet browsing, video games, or shopping, is *expressly for the purpose of creating space to encounter Christ afresh.* That's what sacred waiting does.

The Lenten fast tests those of us who like to pamper ourselves or who have addictive personalities. That covers us all, doesn't it? But the Lord walks with us through this journey.

We ought not to fast and complain. That simply betrays ingratitude and inattention to the Lord. Nor should we fast and boast. Be assured that the ancient Pharisees fasted more regularly and comprehensively than any of us will, and while they felt thoroughly proud of themselves, they remained (for the most part) spiritually deaf and blind to what God was doing. As we fast, we wait humbly, attentively, patiently, consistently, and poised to gratefully serve.

The Lenten fast incorporates small ways of denying ourselves and dying to ourselves that can open doors to rich spiritual growth. And we share this journey with the wider community of faith.

> *Any decision to fast is expressly for the purpose of creating space to encounter Christ afresh.*

For many of us, fasting of any kind simply escapes our radar unless we face a crisis or a time for vital decision making: perhaps forty days for national revival, fourteen days to find a spouse, three days for a career change, and a single meal to decide about refinancing. But the tradition of fasting for forty days before Easter serves at least two helpful purposes. First, it comes around each year and thereby guards us from fasting simply to manipulate God for crisis intervention. Second, it keeps fasting before us as a worthwhile discipline to deepen our hunger and thirst for God.

We won't find Ash Wednesday or Lent in the New Testament. Jesus did not institute them, and Paul didn't write about them. Nevertheless, this season can be deeply meaningful and spiritually enriching.

We need a resurgence in our day of repentance and fasting, in an era when we usually downplay sin and overfeed our appetites. As we consider confession and self-denial, some might say, "I'd rather die!" But that's precisely the point. This fast reenacts a "death" to ourselves so that we might experience a new level of intimacy and "aliveness with Christ." Each time we pine for something we have laid aside for Christ, our mind is briefly drawn to Him afresh.

Sterling Hundley notes: "Fasting is a symbolic act, not a logical act. . . . The symbolism of fasting can be destroyed by too-rigid analysis, or it can be elevated into idolatry. The meaning of fasting is simply our hunger for God and for God's righteousness, expressed with abandon."[5]

"Hunger for God . . . expressed with abandon." Is that not the essence of sacred waiting? We yearn to live in His Presence and be fully present to Him, because in the deepest recesses of our hearts we know that true life flows from Him, not ourselves. Thus in our best moments we want to move past our personal pampering and into personal transformation. We desire to serve Him and not the world. And Lent facilitates this deep longing that wells up within us. It provides a regular and systematic way to minimize some of our own comforts so that we can attend more fully to Him.

We may devise many excuses for not fasting, but ultimately our excuses simply highlight our light appetite for God. One writer puts it this way: "The path to the buffet table and the path to sanctification lie in opposite directions."[6] That may be truer than we want to admit.

Fasting is an ancient spiritual exercise designed to enhance our alertness to God. The Lenten season—marked by thoughtful fasting—calls us to set our minds afresh on Him and to listen harder than usual; perhaps harder than ever.

As we restrain ourselves from a particular indulgence or comfort, we find ourselves much more aware of Christ and far more sensitive to His voice. Jesus said to His disciples, "My sheep hear My voice" (John 10:27 NASB). Lent can certainly sharpen our hearing.

GROUP DISCUSSION

1. Have you ever fasted as a discipline to draw closer to God? If so, what happened? How did you find the experience? What did you learn?

2. If you were to observe Lent—the forty days of fasting—what might you fast from that would be a meaningful sacrifice on your part to emulate the "wilderness experience"?

3. What role do you think solitude plays in our sacred waiting? How can we practice solitude in this crowded world and crowded timetable that we live by?

4. How do you feel about the idea of an annual spiritual spring cleaning? Why might this be a beneficial step toward more authentic sacred waiting?

5. "Repentance and fasting deserve a resurgence in our day, in an era when we usually downplay sin and overfeed our appetites." In our quest to wait more seriously on God, why should we address our sin head on? And why is self-denial so foundational to sacred waiting?

CHAPTER 8

THE EASTER WAIT

Lord, teach me that the journey toward death is but the pathway to eternal resurrection. When I fight for my own rights and interests, grant me the Easter heart, a heart confident in your goodness and provision, a heart that trusts you through the valley of the shadow of death. Amen.

On Wednesday, July 30, 1997, at 11:35 PM—in the middle of the Australian winter—eighteen people died when two ski lodges collapsed in the ski resort of Thredbo, in the Snowy Mountains of Australia. Over three thousand, eight hundred tons of mud and debris, loosened by a leaking water main and an inferior roadway higher on the mountain, roared down the slope and destroyed the lodges that were filled with sleeping skiers.

Police and emergency workers quickly responded to the disaster, facing a highly unstable site in the middle of the night. Medical staff arrived from surrounding townships, and four medical specialists were flown 300 miles from St. George Hospital, in Sydney, to Thredbo. By 2:30 AM, multiple rescue agencies were set up at the site, and the frantic search for survivors was underway. Search and rescue teams recovered the first body at 4:20 PM on Thursday—nearly seventeen hours after the landslide.

The steep slope, the shifting debris, and the freezing conditions made rescue efforts perilous. Additionally, on Thursday night the temperature dropped to seven degrees Fahrenheit. All hope faded quickly for finding survivors buried in the mud beneath the concrete slabs.

On Friday, search teams recovered one more body in the early morning, and two more later that day. With each passing hour, it grew increasingly clear that no one had survived this catastrophic mudslide.

Then at 5:37 AM on Saturday, rescue workers dropped sound equipment into a hole they had dug, as was the standard procedure. But this time, they detected some movement underneath the concrete slab.

Rescue expert Steve Hirst double-checked the monitoring equipment and yelled down the hole: "Rescue team working overhead. Can anyone hear me?" A single voice called back, "I can hear you."

Stuart Diver, a ski instructor, was alive.

Over the next eleven hours, rescuers worked hard to extract Diver from the small cavity between two huge concrete slabs where he lay near the body of his wife, Sally, who had died by drowning more than two days before.

Diver spent sixty-five grueling hours buried under the rubble before he finally emerged late on Saturday evening, freezing cold, wrapped in a blanket, and carried on a stretcher; virtually three days after the burial.[1]

As extraordinary as Stuart Diver's story is, it pales in comparison to the resurrection of Jesus. Jesus spent three days in an authentic tomb after suffering and dying on the barbaric cross. Whipped, beaten, pierced, humiliated, and killed, His death was complete and unequivocal. Yet on the third day, without emergency services personnel crowding around, without doctors and specialists to monitor his life status, God raised Him from the dead. And He walked out of the tomb, not *cheating* death (like Stuart Diver), but *conquering* death for all time.

> *Jesus walked out of the tomb, not cheating death, but conquering death for all time.*

At Easter each year, the church celebrates the resurrection of Jesus Christ from the grave after those three days—not a rescue but a resurrection. But historically the church has recognized the entire week leading up to Easter Sunday. The period between Palm Sunday (recalling the triumphal entry of Jesus into Jerusalem) and Easter Sunday (the resurrection of Jesus from the grave) is commonly called *Holy Week*. And the events in the life of Jesus and His disciples during this Holy Week teach us a great deal about sacred waiting.

THAT FIRST EASTER

Palm Sunday comes the weekend before Easter and commemorates the triumphal entry of Jesus, seated on a donkey, into Jerusalem (John 12:12–15). Many of the people in the crowd that day threw palm branches and articles of clothing onto the road as a sign of their hopes and to honor Jesus. It also signaled the start of the final week of Jesus' life—seven days of discouragement for those who had raised their hopes so high—the seven days that we call Holy Week.

John's gospel devotes nine of its twenty-one chapters to describing the events of that week and appropriately so. The atmosphere was highly charged for the disciples. They knew that Jesus had set His eyes on Jerusalem some time earlier and now the time had come; the watershed moment had almost arrived. Everything about Jesus' life and ministry was about to reach its climax.

The week included Jesus' bold entry into Jerusalem (John 12:12–15), driving the money changers out of the temple (Mark 11:15–18), washing the feet of His disciples (John 13:1–11), sharing the Last Supper with them (Luke 22:14–20), facing the hostile crowd at the betrayal by Judas (Matthew 26:47–56), enduring the false trial and a gruesome crucifixion (Luke 22:66–71; 23:1–49), and then rising from the dead (John 20:1–18). Behind all of these events lay a palpable sense of anticipation. As each event unfolded, the disciples surely wondered, "What next?" With their adrenaline pumping in regular bursts, each event of that Easter week trained them in another important facet of sacred waiting—the reshaping of their Kingdom expectations. As they waited on Jesus—spending the week with Him, listening to Him, and serving Him—He substantially remolded their Kingdom views.

The dramatic entry into Jerusalem fueled the hopes of everyone. Jesus had just raised Lazarus from the dead in an outlying township, and the news had spread quickly (John 11:30–46). His march toward Jerusalem had included multiple miraculous healings, and from the perspective of the disciples, everything was rapidly coming to a head. A showdown seemed imminent. For several years they had walked the dusty roads of Israel with Jesus, waiting for Him to burst out of His obscurity and challenge the powers of the day. Surely that moment had arrived.

But if Jesus raised the expectations of His disciples by entering Jerusalem like the prophesied king (see Zechariah 9:9), He then puzzled them by withdrawing again. He did not organize top-level meetings with governing officials. He did not summon lightning bolts from heaven to smite the Roman garrison. Instead, He made His base at Bethany, a small village community outside Jerusalem, and adopted a low profile—low enough that had the Jewish authorities not been so intent on ending His popularity, and had Judas not later betrayed Jesus, it's quite possible He would not have attracted sufficient attention from the Romans to even get arrested.

The roller coaster ride continued for the disciples. Excitement and adrenaline were followed by confusion, disappointment, and letdown.

Our own journey of faith often rides this same roller coaster. We're confident that we know exactly what God is going to do. He shows up in power one moment, and we're certain that glory and victory are at hand. He will quickly conquer all our rivals and deliver us from oppression or hardship. But then He retreats to Bethany and melts back into relative obscurity.

Perhaps it's conflict in the workplace or conflict in a marriage that we expect Him to sweep in and resolve. Surely He shares our sense of justice and knows how faithful we've been to Him. Surely He will step in and deliver us from evil—the evil that swirls around us like storm clouds. And we sense that He is about to do so, but He seems to fall silent or slip away. It easily discourages us, until we change our perspective.

We need not lose heart. After all, He *will* deliver us. But His timing, method, and manner often seem out of sync with our expectations. He has a timetable of His own, does things in ways we wouldn't expect, and sometimes defines deliverance differently than we do.

We rarely share the divine perspective, and that deficiency within us makes waiting—sacred waiting—all the harder and all the more necessary. In our finiteness we tend to see the world and life from a single perspective and our inability to integrate multiple viewpoints limits us enormously.

In the 2008 movie thriller *Vantage Point,* the attempted assassination of the American president is viewed through the eyes of several people at the scene who each saw the event from a different perspective. The only way to unravel what really happened—and identify the real assailants—was to combine the various viewpoints. Though each character witnessed the assassination attempt, they could not and did not see the whole picture.

That first Easter week included multiple elements hidden from the view of the average onlooker. The disciples could neither predict the course of events, nor hasten their own agenda. God's own plan—infinitely better than anything the ragtag twelve could brainstorm—coalesced all the divine viewpoints into something perfect, something far beyond our capacity or that of the disciples to comprehend.

Do we have sufficient faith to trust God when disaster stands at our door or we are confronted with the unknown or unexpected?

WATCH AND LEARN

As the Easter week unfolded, Jesus taught His disciples and modeled for them a series of fundamental lessons about sacred waiting.

Waiting on God demands integrity and prayer.

According to Matthew's account of the triumphal entry into Jerusalem, as soon as Jesus dismounted the donkey He headed for the temple, not to present a sacrifice but to toss out the merchants and traders who had set up their stalls in the forecourts (Matthew 21:12–17). Their offense was not that they sold animals for sacrifice, but that they ripped off the well-meaning pilgrims in the process.

Here in the nation's most sacred venue, a simple form of extortion had developed. The merchants, financiers, and priests had found a handy way to turn a profit in the name of religion. The temple tax could only be paid in the local currency, which foreigners could acquire by converting their foreign currency—at the temple. The conversion—known as money changing—usually involved outrageous exchange rates and costs, so that a visiting pilgrim could easily end up paying a substantially larger temple tax than a local

Jew. Somewhere along the line, the temple caretakers had quietly turned religion into a profitable business.

As the disciples witnessed Jesus angrily overturning the tables of the money changers and declaring that the Lord's house should be a house of prayer, not for scamming, they knew the coming Kingdom's priorities included integrity and prayer. And as Kingdom priorities, they also become foundational for anyone waiting on the Lord.

If we are serious about drawing near to God and experiencing His empowerment as we serve Him, we cannot diminish or compromise integrity and prayer in our lives. Hypocrisy and prayerlessness—our natural default settings—create a distance between us and the Father and undermine our walk with Him. Thus our capacity to align ourselves with Him, discern His voice, and partner with Him in His mission in the world demands a resolute commitment on our part to integrity and prayer.

Waiting on God requires hearts of service and humility.

Later that week, on "the first day of Unleavened Bread on which the Passover lamb had to be sacrificed" (Luke 22:7 NASB), Jesus gathered His disciples together in an upper room of a home for what we now call the *Last Supper*. After the meal—loaded with significance since it recalled God's deliverance of Israel from Egypt and so many expected that week to usher in God's deliverance of Israel from Rome—Jesus took a basin and towel and washed His disciples' feet. No more menial task existed in the household than to tend the feet of guests, who usually traveled barefoot or with open sandals over dirt roads. And Jesus, on the cusp of fulfilling His destiny in Jerusalem, humbly served the disciples.

The scene shocks us. We expect Him to be pampered in this run-up to the cross. But He seeks no sympathy, makes no excuses, and expects no privileges. He simply serves in the humblest possible way. And He startles His disciples, and us, by adding, "Now that

I, your Lord and Teacher, have washed your feet, you also should wash one another's feet" (John 13:14).

Lest any of us assume that waiting on God entitles us to special considerations, Jesus dispels the idea quickly and completely. Nor does waiting on God justify pride or special status. To the contrary, Christ commands us to embrace the lowliest roles and practice the most menial tasks in service of each other and of Him. Humility and service help form the centerpieces to lives that wait on the Father.

Many of us eventually discover that in our pursuit of glitz and glamour, recognition and significance, power and prestige, we have lost sight not only of the *concept* of waiting on God but also the *capacity* to wait on God. And in reality, some of us *avoid* waiting on Him. Service and humility look so much shabbier than the fleeting glory around us. Nevertheless, in those final few days before Easter, as Jesus seizes the opportunity to spotlight the fundamentals of waiting on God, He models to His disciples the centrality of service, humility, integrity, and prayer.

WAITING WITHOUT VIOLENCE

The violence and brutality of Easter speaks to another core element of waiting on God—the embrace of nonviolence. The cruelty and barbarism of the cross calls us into a Kingdom of exceptional, God-empowered, Spirit-driven, Jesus-like compassion and forgiveness. The hostility on Golgotha, which summoned forth all the demons and darkest forces of the cosmos, wilted in the face of love. It still does, though few of us believe it.

Consider a largely overlooked turning point in that week's drama: the arrest in Gethsemane. Lit only by the full moon and the flickering flames of the hostile crowd, the garden provides a profound Kingdom moment.

In the chaos and adrenaline, Peter whips out a sword and slashes wildly at the nearest person. Malchus, the unfortunate bystander, ducks his head just in time to save his scalp but lose an ear. Then Matthew records Jesus' blazing response.

"Put your sword back into its place; for all those who take up the sword shall perish by the sword" (Matthew 26:52 NASB).

Only Luke, the doctor, mentions that Jesus healed the ear. But this moment in Gethsemane represented the final opportunity for Jesus to resist the looming crucifixion. He could run, fight, or surrender. He chose the latter. And in that choice, He taught a powerful Kingdom truth. As He waits on the Father—to fulfill the Father's will—even in the midst of violence, He does not respond to violence with violence.

"Put your sword back into its place."

The Kingdom of God will not be saved, served, or assisted by violence.

The Kingdom of God will not be saved, served, or assisted by violence. The way of Christ is not the way of aggression.

Surely that first Easter, properly understood, proclaims the senselessness, futility, and godlessness of violence. Yet as Western believers, we continue to nurture a culture of violence. We spend hundreds of millions of dollars[2] and countless hours on violent video games and call it social networking. We patronize graphic movies that dish up gratuitous violence and label it entertainment—even while these choices and habits contradict the essence of Christ's Kingdom. We are increasingly desensitized to violence and embrace it uncritically. More than an embrace, we have so absorbed it into our bloodstream that various forms of aggression in our homes, workplaces, sporting fields, and neighborhoods have become an accepted norm.

As followers of Christ, we have not learned the way of Christ until we learn to wait on the Father without resorting to violence.

SHARING HIS DEATH AND RESURRECTION

We don't talk much about *our* cross. On Good Friday we may give thirty minutes to speak about Jesus on *His* cross. In Communion services we might briefly consider Christ's cross again. But when did you last hear a sermon, listen to a radio host, or read an article that called you to take up your own cross?

Many of us have an utterly deficient theology of the cross—our own cross.

We want our lives to be improved, not transformed. We want the "free gift" (Romans 6:23 NASB) of salvation without the responsibility of dying daily (1 Corinthians 15:31 NASB) to ourselves. We want blessing without duty, grace without obligation, and life without death.

Thomas à Kempis, author of the fifteenth-century spiritual classic *The Imitation of Christ*, observed:

> There will always be many who will love Christ's heavenly kingdom, but few who will bear his cross. Jesus has many who desire consolation, but few who care for adversity. He finds many to share his table, but few will join him in fasting. Many are eager to be happy with him; few wish to suffer anything for him. . . . Many are awed by his miracles; few accept the shame of his cross.[3]

Will we go the second mile with Him?

The paradox of the cross is that we will not find a higher way to follow Him, nor a less exalted one. No other path of faith is so dangerous or so safe, so necessary or so neglected. Yet the cross has collapsed into a sentimental symbol—a mere trinket worn around the neck—rather than our vocation. But crucifixion never stands as an option for the follower of Christ. It is central to the life of faith, and foundational to waiting on the Lord.

> *The cross has collapsed into a sentimental symbol rather than our vocation.*

As important as Jesus' teaching is to our lives, His crucifixion is the focal point of our faith. Then, having accepted the grace extended through the cross, we are crucified with Christ, not in some abstract theological sense but in practical ways every day.

Discipleship, in substantial part, is our commitment to the suffering Christ. We do not merely look on as interested, or even appalled, observers. Rather, we yield our lives to share in His suffering.

As we saw in chapter 5, the apostle Paul abandoned himself completely to Christ and considered all of his achievements as rubbish "that I may gain Christ . . . that I may know Him and the power of His resurrection *and the fellowship of His sufferings, being conformed to His death*; in order that I may attain to the resurrection from the dead" (Philippians 3:8, 10–11 NASB). It's those italicized words that we resist.

The irony is that we will all bear a cross of one sort or another. Perhaps the spiritual lethargy that we feel, our disillusionment with faith, our spiritual impotence, our boredom and frustration, all stem from the misguided pursuit of a costless grace and a deathless life. And this lesser life of shattered dreams, frustrated aspirations, and failed efforts becomes a cross of its own in our lives.

If we genuinely embrace the very death to ourselves that our baptism signifies—death to our own interests, rights, preferences, and needs—we will discover resurrection life in our marriages, families, workplaces, and churches. Easter should teach us this if nothing else. And this cross—His and ours—provides the platform for sacred waiting.

THE SACRAMENT OF PAIN

P. T. Forsyth, an early twentieth-century English preacher and writer, once described pain as a sacrament, something through which God imparts grace to us. He stated:

We pray for the removal of pain, pray passionately, and then with exhaustion, sick from hope deferred and prayer's failure. But there is a higher prayer than that. It is a greater thing to pray for pain's conversion than for its removal. It is more of grace to pray that God would make a sacrament of it. *The sacrament of pain!* God has blessed pain even in causing us to pray for relief from it. . . . Whatever drives us to Him, and even nearer Him, has a blessing in it.[4]

How do we wait on God amidst personal pain? How do we wait on Him when suffering threatens to overwhelm us and everything around us is crumbling? We pray. And we see prayer itself as the answer to our circumstances. We accept our pain and suffering as sharing in the cross of Christ and as sacraments—sources of grace, catalysts for intimacy.

None of this comes easily or quickly. To pray for pain's conversion rather than its removal is to pray in unfamiliar ways. We typically ask the Lord to alleviate the pain rather than transform it, because our eyes remain fixed primarily on this life and not the next. Our narrow focus on what *is* prevents us from receiving what *can be*. And the well-meaning consolations from friends and family that we simply "hang in there" and "this too shall pass" divert us from the potential that lies within the moment. Once again, it demonstrates our limited perspective of life. As we learn to wait on the Father, that perspective broadens and conversion happens. As we wait on Him we find that He "prepare[s] a table before [us] in the presence of [our] enemies" (Psalm 23:5). And the One we wait on waits on us.

Thomas Merton, in an essay titled "The Word of the Cross," wrote:

When I see my trials not as the collision of my life with a blind machine called fate, but as the sacramental gift of Christ's love, given to me by God the Father along with my identity and my very name, then I can consecrate them and myself with them to God. For then I realize that my suffering is not my own. It is the Passion of Christ.[5]

Easter motivates us and enables us to redefine our own ordeals in light of Jesus. Had He not suffered, we might embrace bitterness rather than grace; we'd see only harm and not hope. And our pain could produce sufficient resentment to tear us away from waiting on God. But Jesus' own embrace of the cross enables us to do the same.

As we close this chapter, we've seen that Holy Week challenges us to wait on God with integrity, prayer, service, and humility; to face death with resurrection hope, to refuse to participate in the culture of violence, and to recognize and embrace the sacrament of pain.

Everything about that extraordinary week—the week that changed the world—speaks again of God's timing, God's methods, and God's manner. It looked nothing like what the disciples expected. Indeed, at one point it seemed that the Father's plan had failed. But Easter reminds us that "those who wait on the LORD shall renew their strength; they shall mount up with wings like eagles, they shall run and not be weary, they shall walk and not faint" (Isaiah 40:31 NKJV).

GROUP DISCUSSION

1. Have you ever found that God's timing, methods, and plans differed from your own? Describe a time when you experienced the ups and downs of faith that the disciples experienced in that first Holy Week.

2. How much do the themes of integrity, prayer, service, and humility play out in your own life? How do these

four qualities prepare our hearts to meaningfully wait on God?

3. In what ways does our culture of violence impact our witness for the Kingdom of God and our capacity to wait on God?

4. Discuss ways in which we might "share the sufferings of Christ" and thereby deepen our sensitivity to Him.

5. How might viewing pain as a "sacrament" help you experience the Presence of God differently and serve the Lord differently during seasons of suffering?

CHAPTER 9

THE PENTECOST WAIT

Holy Spirit, come. Come in your fullness and usher in the kingdom of God in fresh ways within my life. Grant me faith to wait on you. Amen.

In the Bible, the number *forty* usually represents a period of testing. It often denotes a season of waiting on God, growing in discernment, dealing with temptation, or a time of purification.

The great flood that destroyed the earth involved unprecedented torrential rains for forty days and nights (Genesis 7:12). Moses spent forty years in the wilderness before the Lord called him to deliver Israel from Egypt (Acts 7:30–34). The spies who scouted out the land of Canaan to see if Israel could occupy it took forty days to make their trip and their infamous assessment (Numbers 13:25). Israel then spent forty years wandering in the wilderness before entering the

Promised Land (Numbers 32:13). During those wanderings, Moses spent forty days on one occasion on the mountain of the Lord, receiving the plans for the tabernacle (Exodus 24:18), and another time to receive the Ten Commandments (Exodus 34:28). Once in the Promised Land, Israel "did evil in the eyes of the Lord," and He gave them into the hands of their enemies, the Philistines, for forty years (Judges 13:1). Goliath, the Philistine giant, later taunted Israel for forty days (1 Samuel 17:16). The great prophet Elijah fasted for forty days (1 Kings 19:8). Jonah preached to Nineveh that they had forty days to repent before God would destroy the great city (Jonah 3:4). Jesus spent forty days in the wilderness before He commenced His ministry (Matthew 4:1–2). The number *forty* crops up repeatedly.

After His resurrection, Luke tells us that Jesus "showed himself to [the disciples] and gave many convincing proofs that he was alive. He appeared to them *over a period of forty days* and spoke about the kingdom of God" (Acts 1:3). Everyone who knows the significance of the number *forty* knows what Luke means here. This period between the resurrection of Jesus and the spectacular birth of the church was a season of testing, purifying, and clarifying. Would the disciples wait on God or take matters into their own hands? Would they draw into His Presence and serve His will, or race out in their own strength and try to start their own movement?

> *Would the disciples wait on God or take matters into their own hands?*

ENTREPRENEURS ON HOLD

Passover—the same time that Jesus was crucified and raised from the dead—celebrated the Lord's deliverance of Israel from Egypt. *Fifty days later,* the calendar marks Pentecost. The Jews had several names for Pentecost, including Feast of Weeks and Shavuot, and originally celebrated God's provision of the early spring harvest at this time (Leviticus 23:15–16).[1] After the resurrection, Jesus appeared to His disciples and various others during the seven weeks between Passover and Pentecost.

If we had followed Jesus in those days, met the risen Christ as He walked on the road to Emmaus, or chatted with Him at the Sea of Galilee, where He issued the Great Commission (Matthew 28:19–20), we'd have been raring to go.

The Kingdom we'd heard about for three years would have seemed closer than ever. We'd have just been through the most heartrending and disillusioning experience of our lives: witnessing the crucifixion of Jesus. But seeing that death itself could not hold Him, our energy levels would have been replenished. Our hope would have abounded once more.

Imagine establishing a committee to plan the next steps of the Kingdom campaign: With no time to lose, there should be a victory parade for the risen Lord, culminating in His entering the temple again. Talk about putting the fear of God into the religious leaders who called for His execution! The grass roots should be mobilized (like with any good political campaign). Stories must be sent out—carefully coordinated media releases, of course—to the villages and cities. Jesus will need to make some strategic appearances. Who will put together His itinerary? How shall we prepare for possible military confrontation with the Romans? So much to do! So many people to tell! We'll mobilize multiple cells of Jesus' followers across the land. Revisit his childhood home in Nazareth to recruit family members. Raise funds. Appoint the apostles in charge of various major elements of the campaign. The speed of our response will determine the success of our endeavor.

But *wait* … Jesus calls us together and says, "Wait!"

It's crazy. We'll lose momentum if we wait. We need to

capitalize on what we have. Wait for what? Time is of the essence. We know this is a winning team.

"Wait!"

Nothing aggravates an entrepreneur more than having to wait. Nothing kills enthusiasm and hype more than dead time. Didn't Jesus know that such an instruction risked killing the movement before it began?

Of course, we don't know if the disciples debated such strategy with Jesus or not. But *we* might have. Indeed, we would have. We do.

Our own entrepreneurial culture—driven by stiff competition and the fear of failure, compelled by the need to seize the day and miss no opportunity—demands strategic thinking and planning. Those who fail to plan, plan to fail, after all. But Pentecost, both the weeks leading up to it and the day itself, reminds us that His ways are higher than our ways and His plans greater than our own, usually more so than we could ask or imagine.

Luke tells us that Jesus gathered His disciples together and commanded them, "Do not leave Jerusalem, but *wait for the gift* my Father promised, which you have heard me speak about" (Acts 1:4).

The disciples had heard Jesus speak about the Holy Spirit, but they surely did not realize the tremendous impetus they'd experience once the Spirit came. So how did they respond?

Luke says they returned to Jerusalem, went to the upper room where they had lodging, and "they all joined together constantly in prayer, along with the women and Mary the mother of Jesus, and with his brothers" (Acts 1:14). They prayed. Constantly. Waiting for the gift of the Spirit did not mean watching time pass by, but waiting on the Father—drawing closer to Him than ever in prayer so they could be more ready than ever for service. They practiced the biblical model of presence and service. And for ten days—from the time Jesus ascended into heaven until the time the Holy Spirit came—120 followers of Jesus prayed earnestly together. For what? For His will to be done and their lives to be used.

WALKING WITH, NOT RUNNING AHEAD

The disciples prayed day after day, giving their hearts and ears to the Father. They could not have imagined what "the gift of the Holy Spirit" would mean, nor did they know when the gift would be given, but they knew that the best way to prepare was to pray and wait.

The Holy Spirit had empowered military rulers in Israel's past and loosened the tongues of prophets throughout Israel's history, but under the old covenant, the gift had only been for the elite and the few. The Spirit had come upon various select individuals but never inhabited common folk. So nobody could have anticipated what was to happen on the day of Pentecost, when the Lord poured out His Spirit on the disciples and about three thousand others who decided to follow Jesus.

As one person after another repented of their sins and was baptized in the name of Jesus, the Father birthed the church. And every believer received the promised gift of the Holy Spirit. It was a phenomenal day, not because the apostles had orchestrated it beautifully but because they had opened their hearts and lives to whatever the Lord wanted to do. And He did it!

Fifteen to twenty years later, the apostle Paul wrote to churches in Galatia, reminding the believers who tended to live in their old ways that they were to "walk by the Spirit" (Galatians 5:16 NASB), be "led by the Spirit" (v. 18 NASB), and "follow the Spirit's leading" (v. 25 NLT). In other words, key to the effective Christian life is "walking with" rather than "running ahead." Waiting on God, like waiting on tables, means staying alongside, not blazing our own trail.

Many of us live life with a take-charge attitude and extend that to our relationship with Christ. If He's silent, we assume we're free to plow ahead. If it's moral and legal, then we have no impediment. Many of us adopt the attitude that it is Jesus' duty to stop us rather than lead us. What could be more contrary to the lesson of Pentecost and the teaching of Paul?

Walking by the Spirit, being led by the Spirit, and following the Spirit all imply a very different attitude, which reflects the prayerful sensitivity of the early apostles as they gathered together "continually devoting themselves . . . to prayer" (Acts 2:42 NASB) before *and after* Pentecost. It reflects the prayerful attentiveness of Peter and John as they went to the temple to pray and a certain lame man begged them for alms (see Acts 3:2 KJV). We can well imagine many beggars around the temple area, but a certain one caught their eye, and the Lord performed a miraculous healing that would fill the onlookers with wonder and amazement. "Following the Spirit" reflects the prayerful awareness that the Father might want to do or say something through us in a particular encounter with a particular person.

For many of us, such waiting on the Lord—such attentiveness, walking, following, and serving—would mean a radical shift from our usual approach to the Father. We might describe it as "the Pentecostal shift"—not in the sense of tongues, signs, and wonders, but in the sense of attentiveness, awareness, and responsiveness. If we choose to manage our own lives, follow our own agenda, or simply neglect the Spirit's plan and purpose, we'll find ourselves engaged in futility, frustration, stress, and eventual burnout. Can we slow down sufficiently to walk with Him? And will we be attentive to Him? The day of Pentecost models the priority and power of prayerful attentiveness.

RESTORATION

Pentecost also speaks wonderfully of our restoration when we "wait on the Lord." There's a story behind the birth of the church, and it involves the apostle Peter.

Peter's story provides a roller coaster ride: successful in business, brawny from his days as a fisherman, a natural leader, and then the recipient of divine revelation. When Jesus asked the disciples who they thought He was, Peter provided the $100,000 answer: "You are the Christ, the Son of the living God" (Matthew 16:16). Jesus commended him with an ego-stroking affirmation and gave him a wonderful privilege:

> "Blessed are you, Simon son of Jonah, for this was not revealed to you by man, but by my Father in heaven. And I tell you that you are Peter, and on this rock I will build my church, and the gates of Hades will not overcome it. I will give you the keys of the kingdom of heaven; whatever you bind on earth will be bound in heaven, and whatever you loose on earth will be loosed in heaven."
>
> Matthew 16:17–19

Revelation, renaming, and reward! How does someone keep their head and remain humble in the face of all that? Peter evidently couldn't. From that mountaintop high he plunged into a deep valley of embarrassment and confusion, recorded *just four verses later* in Matthew's gospel. Jesus began to tell His disciples that He must suffer and die, and Peter rebuked Jesus for even suggesting such a thing.

Now that Peter held the keys to the Kingdom of God, he probably felt duty-bound to advise Jesus that negative talk wouldn't build a strong support base. "Jesus turned and said to Peter, 'Get behind me, Satan! You are a stumbling block to me; you do not have in mind the things of God, but the things of men.'" (Matthew 16:23). In a heartbeat Peter fell from gatekeeper of the Kingdom to a self-centered tool of Satan. It wasn't his only slip.

Following the Last Supper, as Judas set about making contact with the Jewish authorities to betray Jesus, Peter was swept away once again with false bravado. As Jesus got up to head out into the dark night, Peter declared, "I will lay down my life for you" (John 13:37). But before dawn broke on the new day, Peter ran scared from the garden of Gethsemane, abandoning Jesus (Mark 14:50) and then "followed him at a distance" as the Roman authorities hauled Jesus off to the courtyard of Caiaphas (Mark 14:54).

Then came his lowest point of all: In a series of confrontations with a couple of servant girls and a few other casual onlookers, after Jesus' arrest, Peter denied Christ three times (Mark 14:66–72). Within hours, and with a devastating sense of déjà vu, Peter promised to die for Jesus and then utterly abandoned Him.

Fast-forward to one of the most moving scenes in the New Testament. Jesus has risen from the dead, and within the forty days of testing and clarification for the disciples, Jesus appears again to them at the Sea of Galilee.

As John tells the story, seven of the disciples—those who used to make their living from fishing—had evidently returned to their old stomping ground.[2] In the early morning, as the men returned from their night's efforts, Jesus stood on a beach and called out to them. With the day just dawning and their eyes a little bleary, Jesus remained somewhat indistinguishable in the distance. He had built a small fire and prepared some breakfast, and when He called out across the water, eventually John recognized Jesus and said to Peter, "It is the Lord!" (John 21:7).

We can feel the awkwardness of that moment for Peter. He feels ashamed. Perhaps part of him hoped never to have to face Jesus again. Now here He was, and Peter had no place to run or hide.

The Bible tells us that instead of diving into the bottom of the boat and burying himself beneath the nets, Peter put on his outer garment and leapt into the sea to swim the hundred yards to shore—and to Jesus.

What did they say to each other? It would seem, very little. Peter knew that he had failed Jesus multiple times. He had no excuses and no one to blame. Perhaps he sat quietly, waiting for

Jesus to berate him. But Jesus simply took the fish and the bread He had cooked and served it to the disciples.

Then, after they finished eating, it happened. Jesus looked directly at Peter and began to speak. But His words surely took everyone by surprise.

"Simon, son of John, do you love me?"

Jesus had reverted to Peter's old name—Simon—which means "reed," that which is moved easily by the wind and the water. Could Peter answer the question affirmatively? He'd look like a total hypocrite after what he had done to Jesus. He'd better not claim to *love* Jesus. "Yes, Lord; you know that I think of you fondly."

We might imagine the other disciples watching and holding their breath. What might Jesus say or do now? He had Peter squirming and completely ashamed. Would He ridicule him? Would Jesus curse Peter as He had cursed the hypocritical Pharisees at various times during His ministry? At the very least, they expected Jesus to cast Peter aside. How could He use Peter after he had proven himself so fickle and unreliable? Then the tension of the moment was broken with three short words: "Feed my lambs."

Again Jesus asked the same question. Peter gave the same response. And Jesus said "Take care of my sheep."

A third time Jesus asked the question, but modified it just a little: "Simon, son of John, do you think of me fondly?" Peter dared not muster bravado at this point and offer more than he could deliver. And grieved by the questions but no doubt stunned by the grace Christ extended him, he replied, "Lord, you know all things, you know that I think of you ever so fondly." And Jesus said a third time "Feed my sheep" (see John 21:15–17).[3]

When Peter deserved to be put on the bench, Jesus received him back on the team; restored him back to ministry. When Peter could not expect to get a pew, Jesus offered him the pulpit once again. Grace abounded. Thus less than seven weeks later, on the day of

Pentecost, Peter—the same one who had denied Christ and cursed Him during the trial—stood boldly before thousands of Jews in the temple area and declared the gospel to them, the truth about Jesus, and how they could be reconciled to God (Acts 2:14–41). He also received the promised and transforming gift of the Holy Spirit.

Pentecost represented the pinnacle of restoration for Peter. And it speaks of our restoration, too.

Those who wait upon the Lord shall be restored, even from their deepest shame and failure. If we will draw near to Him and devote our lives to Him (wait on Him), He will receive us. Whatever we may have done to defy or deny God, to hurt or harm others, to abandon or neglect Jesus, none of us is ever beyond the reach of grace. And the day of Pentecost bears testimony to that truth. God makes restoration and transformation His business. Our guilt never exceeds His grace. Our failures never surpass His forgiveness or minimize His fondness for us. Our shame does not stop His steadfast love.

Whatever we may have done to defy or deny God, to hurt or harm others, to abandon or neglect Jesus, none of us is ever beyond the reach of grace.

Those who wait upon the Lord, who sit quietly around the breakfast fire on the beach with Christ, find forgiveness, hope, and restoration. Pentecost confirms it.

SPIRITUAL GIFTS

We usually associate the day of Pentecost with the extraordinary outpouring of spiritual gifts. The disciples had remained in Jerusalem as Jesus instructed them, and when the Lord's appointed time arrived, all manner of spectacular things took place. Little wonder, then, that the contemporary evangelical church—shaking

itself from a drowsiness that descended upon it in the early twentieth century—should hunger for a Pentecostal outpouring again
in our time, whatever that might mean or look like.

As a young pastor, I understood the benefit of spiritual gifts—not
so much my own as those within other people—but from a different perspective. If I could identify those gifts and convince folks
that exercising their gifts would bring meaning and value to their
lives, I'd be able to recruit them more easily for the various church
ministries—and the sooner the better. As a church planter in desperate
need of volunteers, I quickly set about creating my own "Spiritual
Gifts Inventory" to help determine the strengths of people so I could
plug them in to the right places. No need to procrastinate or prolong
this opportunity for significance, I told them sincerely. Their spiritual
gifts held the key to their sense of self-worth and belonging.

I could not have been more misguided.

Since the 1970s, many churches have emphasized the need for
believers to explore their spiritual gift possibilities, to experiment
with various options, to examine their effectiveness, and expect
confirmation from others. With a deft sleight of hand we have
asked people to open their neatly wrapped spiritual packages and
get to work, and have convinced them that this is all biblical and
spiritually beneficial. But the fruit of this approach to Christian
living has not ripened very well.

A few years ago, looking at my bulging file of the various spiritual gifts inventories, I began to realize their weaknesses. Every
inventory depends on the biases and interpretation of the inventory maker. I added music and youth ministry to the gifts from
the apostle Paul's lists in Romans 12 and 1 Corinthians 12, and
even provided my own definitions of each biblical gift. Those dear
people who took my inventories—or anyone's—probably didn't
realize all the bias inherent in an inventory.[4]

Furthermore, every spiritual gifts inventory basically builds on our preexisting strengths and competencies. The questions invariably steer us to identify what we naturally do well, what others affirm in us, what we enjoy, and what seems effective. It does not necessarily identify what God would like to do *super*naturally through us in a given moment. If anything, some inventories simply spiritualize our natural tendencies.

Finally, many of us participate in gifts inventories because we want to know how we fit into the Kingdom of God. We're looking for affirmation and significance. Some pastors even promote the inventories as a way to "discover your place in the Kingdom." But while the secular world connects significance with performance, the Kingdom of God never does. We're important in God's eyes not because we are "doing our job" but because we are His children. Subtly and destructively, spiritual gifts inventories can turn our attention from His love to our efforts.

> *Spiritual gifts inventories can turn our attention from His love to our efforts.*

One observation we can make from the story of Pentecost is that none of the apostles took inventories, examined gift options, or experimented in preparation for "the big day." They didn't need to.

DEFINING AND EXPERIENCING SPIRITUAL GIFTS

A spiritual gift is any ability or activity empowered by the Holy Spirit and blessed by the Father to draw people closer to Christ.[5] And those spiritual gifts are *through* us, not *to* us.

The apostle Paul reminded the Corinthians that we receive empowerment and enabling from the Holy Spirit "for the common good," not for our own good (1 Corinthians 12:7). God blesses others through us. A word of wisdom is not for us but for others *through* us. The same is true of miracles, hospitality, administration, teaching, and healing. The goal of a spiritual gift, in every instance, is not to impress onlookers but to steer them closer to Jesus.

From this perspective, if our actions need no supernatural empowerment or if they fail to draw people closer to Christ, how can we say that we have extended a *spiritual* gift? Consider preaching and teaching, for example. If it fails to be empowered by the Spirit and blessed by the Father to draw us closer to the Son, then it might be a good lecture, useful advice, or an entertaining speech, but the spiritual gifts the Bible speaks of may not be involved at all.

Interestingly, Jesus had little to say in the Gospels about spiritual gifts. Yes, He healed, performed miracles, cast out demons, and modeled various gifts, but He did not instruct His disciples to discover their gifts and exercise them. He did not hand around inventories for the disciples to complete and tabulate. Rather, He taught them to depend upon the Holy Spirit in the moment of need, whatever that need might be (see Luke 12:12). Herein lies the essence of sacred waiting: following the lead of the Holy Spirit. Will we wait on the Lord, trusting Him to minister adequately through us, or will we seek to make ourselves adequate for every task? Paul wrote, "Not that we are adequate in ourselves to consider anything as coming from ourselves, but *our adequacy is from God*" (2 Corinthians 3:5 NASB).

We've grown altogether too self-centered in our discussions (and pursuit) of spiritual gifts. Biblically speaking, God gives gifts through us to build up others—not only to make them feel good but to help them experience His reality. That's what it means to build up the body. That's what we see happening on the day of Pentecost in Acts 2. And that's the essence of sacred waiting. As we wait upon the Lord, He ministers through us to bring others to that place of His Presence, where they might learn to wait upon Him themselves.

GIVEN AS NEEDED

Spiritual gifts represent the Spirit's empowerment for a specific ministry opportunity. In the book of Acts, Peter exercised leadership (1:15). He also emerged as an apostolic figure and an evangelist (2:37–41), and experienced tongues (2:4), prophecy (2:14–36), signs and wonders (2:43), and healing (3:6–7)—all before the fourth chapter! Each circumstance required that God work differently through him, and Peter was willing for that. Indeed, that sensitivity and willingness marked two vital facets of a heart given to sacred waiting.

The Father consistently equips us for the need of the moment if we remain alert, yielded, and sensitive to Him—as we wait on Him. As we walk by the Spirit, He also guides us to people and situations for which He equips us. Inventories tend to restrict us or even make us reluctant to serve at times: "You need healing? That's not my gift!" Well, of course not. God is the healer and the other person is the recipient. At best we serve as simple conduits for God to work through, *if we are willing.*

Spiritual gifts function like tools in God's toolbox. The best tool is the one that is needed! If we're going to pound nails, the best tool will be a hammer, not a saw. If we're going to cut a small hole, we'd best get a drill, not a level. Similarly, healing or prophecy is no greater than wisdom or hospitality or leadership. The best gifts are the gifts needed at the moment. The Father pulls out the most appropriate tool and applies it to others through us if we allow Him.

Ultimately, we best discover spiritual gifts in service, not surveys. As we step out in response to God's leading, we find that His Spirit empowers us in ways we never imagined, the Father blesses us (and others through us) in ways we never expected, and people encounter Christ in deeper ways than ever before.

The season of Pentecost reminds us not to jump ahead of

God but to wait until the promised gift—the Holy Spirit—directs our paths. We don't establish His Kingdom. He does. We don't decide whom to reach out to and when. He does. We don't equip each other for the task of ministry. He does. And as we wait on Him—prayerfully attentive, alert, responsive—He accomplishes His purposes in others through us.

GROUP DISCUSSION

1. How can we curb our tendency to take charge?

2. Do we, like the disciples, have sufficient confidence in prayer to see it as essential, even when we sense there's a job to be done?

3. Describe a time when you have "run ahead" rather than "walked with" God. Why do we find "walking by the Spirit" so difficult at times? What factors make us want to run on ahead?

4. "Those who wait upon the Lord, who sit quietly around the breakfast fire on the beach with Christ, find forgiveness, hope, and restoration. Pentecost confirms it." Do you know someone who needs such a time with Christ?

5. Spiritual gifts—perhaps most dramatically associated with Pentecost—are the tools we need when we need them, not for our own benefit, but for the good of others. And we don't determine which tool is most needed; the Lord does. How does this affect your view of service/ministry and sacred waiting?

CHAPTER 10

THE KINGDOM WAIT

Lord of heaven and earth, may your Kingdom come and your will be done on earth as it is in heaven. When I want to force the coming of that Kingdom, grant me patience and faith in you. When I'm tempted to supplant your Kingdom with my own, teach me to seek your Kingdom above all else. Amen.

I have a friend who pole-vaulted in high school. I never did, nor did I ever want to. The object of the event is to clear a bar placed at a dangerous height by racing down a short, narrow track, planting a long pole into a tiny box fixed at the end of the track, bending the pole to the breaking point, and being catapulted over the bar, all the while trying not to look terror-stricken.

If you're good at it, you'll soar over the high bar and fall easily onto the soft mats on the other side. If you make a mistake or miss the mats . . . ouch!

As Tim recounted his experience, he made a telling observation:

"Once that pole is bent to its capacity and your arms are being yanked out of their sockets, the crucial thing is to relax and just let the pole spring you upward."

Relax? I'd be gripping that pole for dear life.

Tim struggled, too. At that critical moment when his work was done and he needed to relax, he would jerk downward just a little bit more, and periodically break his vaulting pole. That's a good time to take up "virtual vaulting" on the Wii.

In many ways, this parallels our spiritual lives and our desire for the Kingdom of God to come.

Our efforts to reach greater heights with the Father seem too often to end in broken poles. We charge down the track with fresh resolve to read more of the Bible, to journal more often, to pray longer, and to serve with greater commitment. Then we press even harder, believing that intimacy with God and the success of the Kingdom both depend upon extra effort from us. And something snaps. Many of us know the frustration and emptiness of trying to manipulate God. He does not respond to our formulas, demands, or heavy-handedness.

> *The Lord does not respond to our formulas, demands, or heavy-handedness.*

At the very moment when we feel tempted to force God's Presence or Kingdom plan, the biblical witnesses remind us to simply experience it. It's called *remaining,* not straining. Jesus said,

> "Remain in me, and I will remain in you. No branch can bear fruit by itself; it must remain in the vine. Neither can you bear fruit unless you remain in me. I am the vine; you are the branches. If a man remains in me and I in him, he will bear much fruit; apart from me you can do nothing."
>
> John 15:4–5

It's tough for us to wait on God (to "abide" or "remain") in a world that waits for nothing. But *strain* and *drain* should not become honorable words in the Christian quest for divine intimacy or Kingdom effectiveness. "The crucial thing is to relax and just let the pole spring you upward." That surely means, at some point, that we relinquish our dreams, ambitions, determination, and control to God. Rather than view life as a series of crazily high bars to conquer, we discover the joy of the Father lifting us in ways that we could never lift ourselves. We also discover, in waiting on Him, that He builds His Kingdom. We don't work *for* Him. At the very best, we work *with* Him.

Joni Eareckson Tada notes, "It is a glorious thing to know that your Father God makes no mistakes in directing or permitting that which crosses the path of your life. It is the glory of God to conceal a matter. It is our glory to trust Him, no matter what."[1]

NOTHING NEW

The first-century Jews desperately wanted "the Kingdom" to come. After centuries of life on the wrong end of poverty, oppression, fear, and aggression, the Kingdom of God sounded very attractive. No wonder that when Jesus came healing the blind and the lame, casting out demons, and raising the dead, they wanted to take Him by force to make Him king (see John 6:15). Anything they could do to force the coming of the Kingdom seemed good. Indeed, knowing the desperation and intentions of the people around Him, Jesus once noted, "From the days of John the Baptist until now, the kingdom of heaven has been forcefully advancing, and forceful men lay hold of it" (Matthew 11:12). At least that's what they wanted to do.

Judas probably serves as the quintessential example of this hunger to force the Kingdom into existence. With a weak spot for money (he repeatedly pilfered funds from the disciples' money bag—John 12:6) and probably a longing to see the Kingdom of God established in power, he conspired with the Jewish chief priests and elders to hand Jesus over to them for thirty silver coins (see Matthew 26:14–16). He had a clear agenda and his own clear timetable. He'd seen the constant signs and wonders Jesus performed. He probably witnessed the stilling of the storm and the feeding of the thousands. If he could lure the Jewish authorities and Roman garrison into conflict with Jesus, it would force Jesus' hand.

In many ways, Judas may have interpreted his actions as a favor to Israel. In a single strategic step—betrayal—he'd financially profit as well as get credit for the coup that the people longed for. The plan seemed foolproof, except that Judas wanted to seize the Kingdom forcefully, and God's Kingdom will not yield to force. His sovereignty will not be compromised or shared.

Many of us walk the same path as Judas. We may not seize the Kingdom forcefully, but in our churches we organize revivals, concerts, and big events where we expect Him to appear and astonish the audience. We attend conferences, consult the experts, and run programs that have been successful in other churches and expect the Kingdom of God to break out where we live. We study church growth principles and analyze our congregational statistics. We profile the community and produce targeted mailings. We hire staff with a good track record in other places and start programs that have "worked" elsewhere. In short, we desperately want to seize the Kingdom and make it happen. And there's all manner of pressure both within and around us to succeed. Hurting and fearful people can demand a lot. And our quest for the Kingdom may produce the Moses Syndrome.

THE MOSES SYNDROME

When Israel left captivity in Egypt, they quickly faced a severe water shortage. At Rephidim their thirst grew intense, and they demanded that Moses give them water. We're not talking about finding a few bottles of Evian. Israel probably numbered over two million people at that time. Numbers 2:32 indicates there were 603,550 fighting men, not counting the women, children, or aged. And the Lord said to Moses, "I will stand there before you by the rock at Horeb. Strike the rock, and water will come out of it for the people to drink" (Exodus 17:6). Moses did as he was instructed— what a wild idea, to strike a rock—and the Lord caused water to pour forth miraculously, sufficient for everyone and their livestock.

Some time later, Israel faced another parched period. Once again the people came and complained to Moses.

> The LORD said to Moses, "Take the staff, and you and your brother Aaron gather the assembly together. *Speak to that rock* before their eyes and it will pour out its water. You will bring water out of the rock for the community so they and their livestock can drink." So Moses took the staff from the LORD's presence, just as he commanded him. He and Aaron gathered the assembly together in front of the rock and Moses said to them, "Listen, you rebels, must we bring you water out of this rock?" Then *Moses raised his arm and struck the rock* twice with his staff. Water gushed out, and the community and their livestock drank. But the LORD said to Moses and Aaron, "Because you did not trust in me enough to honor me as holy in the sight of the Israelites, you will not bring this community into the land I give them."
>
> Numbers 20:7–12

What a horrifying moment. The Lord instructed Moses to *speak to the rock,* but Moses thought he knew the formula. He had worked out in his own mind how to force the hand of God and make the Kingdom come. You don't speak to the rock, you strike it. So strike he did—and he struck himself out of an inheritance in the Promised Land.

We *should* feel passionate about the gospel and the Kingdom of God. But how easily we forget that the shape, the impact, the timing, and the effectiveness of the Kingdom of God among us comes by the Lord's hand, not our own. Before we seek to apply old formulas or personal preferences, let's wait on the Lord prayerfully, attentively, even urgently. All too often and all too quickly we prefer to mimic others or to simply do it our way.

At conferences and seminars we listen to success stories and long to have a similar story of our own. Veterans of such motivational events wisely advise us to apply the principles but not necessarily the same practices. That's fine and true, but do they neglect to mention waiting on God? It seems that prayerfulness in leadership is often a distant consideration. None of us need wait on God to inaugurate His Kingdom among us when we have the capacity to launch some version of that Kingdom in our own strength.

The Moses Syndrome lures us into self-confidence. It lulls us into believing—based on what we have seen in another place at another time—that we know what's best, and therefore we either ignore or resist any direction of God to the contrary.

Mike, a friend of mine, pastors a church in Southern California. At one time as an associate pastor, his job description was very simple: travel to major Christian conferences around the country every three or four months, gather the best ideas, return to the church and implement those ideas. For several years Mike did as directed but with a brewing sense of discontent. The latest programs rarely captured the imagination of the people, generally failed to inspire them, and lasted only until the next conference and the next idea. At some point Mike turned afresh to prayer and attentiveness to Christ—waiting on Him—and the congregation underwent some profound transformation. Instead of looking beyond themselves for ideas and inspiration, congregational members started asking the Lord to work from within. Gradually people started feeling a burden for one area of ministry or another and began to step forward not only as participants but as potential leaders. And the church has experienced the delight of God's leading, timing, and providing as people discovered His call and conviction within their own lives.

A GARDEN

When did we start to view the Kingdom of God in manufacturing terms rather than organic terms, as a business instead of a garden?

In manufacturing, we build our widgets, perfect them, create a market, sell our products, build our capital, float public shares, organize takeovers and mergers, and exist for wealth creation. We measure our effectiveness according to the capital we acquire: property, facilities, inventory, and cash reserves.

In manufacturing, we report regularly to the board or the stockholders, who expect tangible results, improved products, expanded product lines, and a healthy bottom line. But the Kingdom of God is distinctively organic. It corresponds more to a *biological* plant than a *factory* plant. It incorporates people, not machinery. It embraces cooperation, not competition. And the bottom line is not cash, but Christ.

> The Kingdom of God is distinctively organic. It corresponds more to a biological plant than a factory plant.

Let's not underestimate the implications of such a shift in metaphor. When we discard the *industry* model and embrace the *garden* model, we discover some remarkable freedoms.

First, we don't generally assess gardens by the criteria "bigger is better." While we may marvel at acres of gorgeous landscaping, we can delight just as much in a small plot well-kept. Second, we may diligently tend a garden and attempt to control the environment, but we can't force growth. That's the Gardener's job (see 1 Corinthians 3:6). Have you ever dumped ten times the recommended fertilizer on your lawn to make it green overnight? It burns the grass rather than nourishes it. We can't hurry up organic processes—at least, not much. Finally, organic entities have natural life cycles, where decline and death is normal, not shameful. The Gardener holds a shed full of options when it's time to plant again.

Jesus chose metaphors and parables for the Kingdom from the agricultural context of His day: seed being sown, grain and tares, mustard seeds, and fig trees. Was He simply accommodating the agrarian culture of His day? Or might He still use such images to move us away from "God the Industrialist" to "God the Gardener"? I suspect the latter.

The manufacturing model for the church reduces people to either salesmen or customers and assumes that accumulation signifies success. It demands quarterly reports and clear job descriptions (spiritual gifts). But the organic Kingdom of God confronts such spiritual capitalism. And by doing so, it frees us.

Of course, this Kingdom metaphor presumes that we learn the art of waiting; knowing, like the wise farmer, when to hold back and when to step quickly forward. We've all seen the curiosity of a child who can't resist knowing what's happening inside a cocoon or just under the ground. They tear open the silk chamber or uproot a seedling that has barely broken the surface. Perhaps our enthusiasm—and spiritual immaturity—produces the same destructive results at times.

PROVISION FOR HIS KINGDOM

In January 2009, many American churches and parachurch organizations faced severe economic challenges. Constituents were giving less because they were earning less, if they had jobs at all. And many boards had a knee-jerk rather than a knee-bend reaction. Staff layoffs, program reductions, event cancellations, and even church closures increased alarmingly. The most common reaction was data analysis, strategic planning, and ministry prioritization.

What matters most? What can we afford? What guarantees our survival? The industrial model reflected its grip among us. Not that we should be careless, frivolous, or overly pious, but might the Head of the church have had something to say to the church in those days? Only those willing to wait on Him specifically, intentionally, and consistently in crisis could answer that question.

Shortly after Dallas Theological Seminary was founded in 1924, it almost folded. At the point of bankruptcy and with creditors ready to foreclose at twelve noon on a particular day, the founders of the school met urgently that very morning in the president's office to pray that God would provide. In that prayer meeting was Dr. Harry Ironside. When it came his turn to pray, he said candidly, "Lord, we know you own the cattle on a thousand hills. Please sell some of them and send us the money."

Just about that very time, a tall Texan strolled into the school's business office and told the secretary, "I just sold two carloads of cattle over in Fort Worth. I've been trying to make a business deal go through, but it just won't work. I feel God wants me to give this money to the seminary. I don't know if you need it or not, but here's the check." And he handed it over.

The secretary, knowing the critical nature of the hour, went to the door of the prayer meeting and timidly tapped. Dr. Lewis Sperry Chafer, the founder and president of the school, answered the door and took the check from her hand. It was for the exact sum of the debt. He recognized the name on the check as that of the cattleman, then turned to Dr. Ironside and said, "Harry, God sold the cattle."[2]

It's tough to trust the Kingdom of God to God. Because we belong to it, we assume it's our business to build and sustain it. Dr. Chafer could so easily have spent that morning calling banks, making last-ditch appeals to constituents, and trying to strike deals with creditors—actions he had certainly taken in the preceding months. And those would not have been bad choices. But the best choice lay in faith—faith that the Lord's Kingdom is the Lord's responsibility. As we trust God with the future, we must also realize that while the Father promises us eternity, He doesn't promise our organizations the same. However, the decline or demise of one entity is not the death of the Kingdom of God.

Jesus declared to His disciples (who would have liked some "Kingdom forcefulness," too): "I will build my church, and the gates of Hades will not overcome it" (Matthew 16:18).

Our view of the Kingdom deeply impacts our capacity to wait on the King.

WHY?

The Lord does not miraculously pay all debts to preserve all Christian organizations, nor does He shield us as individuals from all suffering just because we belong to His Kingdom. Those of us who belong to the Kingdom of God can find waiting on God a tough assignment. Many of us experience the anguish of the ancient psalmist:

> "My God, my God, why have you forsaken me? Why are you
> so far from saving me, so far from the words of my groaning?
> O my God, I cry out by day, but you do not answer, by night,
> and am not silent."
>
> Psalm 22:1–2

Entering the Kingdom does not isolate us from the pain and suffering of the world.

In January 1994, doctors diagnosed my wife, Kim, with cancer. The turmoil of our schedule over the next six months of treatment matched the inner turmoil of our souls as we wrestled with age-old questions. Is this God's punishment for something we have done? Or discipline? Or a test? Or just something that happens in a fallen world?

We've had plenty of opportunities since then to ask the questions again, and over time I've drawn the following conclusions.

First, under the new covenant, I'm not sure God punishes very often this side of the grave. He's not in the business of dealing out retribution for its own sake, and the proliferation of evil suggests that He stays His hand far more often than not.

Second, we know that the Father disciplines those He loves (Hebrews 12:6). Could our hardship fall under this category? Absolutely. But no good parent disciplines his child without a clear explanation. An unexpected and unexplained smack on the backside serves no purpose but to confuse a child. It fails to train him. Similarly, the Father's discipline will always have a clear reason and origin.

Our third possibility is a "test." The Bible tells us that the Lord tested Abraham (Hebrews 11:17–18). Perhaps our suffering falls in this category. But remember, God never tests us to defeat us. His tests have a single purpose: to build us up. Satan, by contrast, tempts us to harm us. Ultimately, we can only discern a test with hindsight.

How then should we evaluate our pain or suffering?

Punishment is so rare we can virtually rule it out. If we see no clear cause and effect, we can also dismiss the likelihood of discipline. And since a test is best assessed in hindsight, we're left with just one authentic option: Persist in faith in the midst of a fallen world. Wait on the Lord with sincerity and earnestness, even though the question *Why?* remains unanswered.

Faith in His goodness is our best response. The Kingdom does not shield us from hardship or offer us safe haven from grief, much as we might like it to. And those who understand that the Kingdom of God is not a place but a way of living understand that waiting on the Father in plenty and in want reflects a fundamental Kingdom value.

It's natural to ask *Why?* We all do it. But for those who follow Christ, the more important question to eventually ask is *How?* How shall we draw nearer to Him and express our trust in Him despite the chaos in which we find ourselves, whether His Kingdom has broken through or not?

Then perhaps we shall declare with the psalmist after his anguished cry in Psalm 22:1–2, the next three verses of that same psalm: "Yet you are enthroned as the Holy One. . . . In you our fathers put their trust; they trusted and you delivered them. They cried to you and were saved; in you they trusted and were not disappointed" (Psalm 22:3–5).

IT'S GOD'S KINGDOM

In the Sermon on the Mount, Jesus encourages us to seek first God's Kingdom and His righteousness, and He'll take care of all the daily needs that we usually spend our time worrying about—food, clothing, and shelter (Matthew 6:31–33). When we read that text, our attention usually dwells on God's provision, and we skip lightly over the fact that it is God's *Kingdom* that we seek, not His provision. Somewhere deep within us, perhaps because God created us to rule and to reign,[3] we want to make His Kingdom our kingdom. In our brokenness, we seek to control His Kingdom rather than conform to it. If we seek His Kingdom at all, it's primarily to expand our own.

> *In our brokenness, we seek to control His Kingdom rather than conform to it.*

Whose kingdom do we really seek?

When we seek first the Kingdom of God, it's not that we can

then seek second our own kingdom, as though both are legitimate pursuits. Rather, we seek His Kingdom above anything else, and our kingdom gradually fades entirely from the picture. Inevitably that means living in His Kingdom, His way. It requires a radical shift in our priorities and preferences. We don't call the shots in His Kingdom, He does. Our first duty, then, is attentiveness to Him. We wait on Him.

Jesus shared some parables with His disciples that drove home this same point. Consider the following:

> "The kingdom of heaven is like a man who sowed good seed in his field. But while everyone was sleeping, his enemy came and sowed weeds among the wheat, and went away. When the wheat sprouted and formed heads, then the weeds also appeared.
>
> "The owner's servants came to him and said, 'Sir, didn't you sow good seed in your field? Where then did the weeds come from?'
>
> "'An enemy did this,' he replied.
>
> "The servants asked him, 'Do you want us to go and pull them up?'
>
> "'No,' he answered, 'because while you are pulling the weeds, you may root up the wheat with them. Let both grow together until the harvest. At that time I will tell the harvesters: First collect the weeds and tie them in bundles to be burned; then gather the wheat and bring it into my barn.'"
>
> Matthew 13:24–30

When the disciples later asked Jesus the meaning of the parable, he highlighted the impatience we may have to "clean up" God's Kingdom, wanting to decide who's in and who's out, wanting to jump in and pull out the weeds. But Jesus reminded them—and us—that the Father will judge the hearts in due course. He never abdicates the throne of His Kingdom, though we may try and sit on it ourselves from time to time. It always has been and always will be His Kingdom. Meanwhile, will we wait on Him, attend to Him, respond to Him, or seek to usurp Him?

═══════════ GROUP DISCUSSION ═══════════

1. What does Jesus mean when He says, "Apart from me you can do nothing" (John 15:5)? How does this connect with waiting on Him?

2. Describe some examples of the Moses Syndrome that you have seen in your own life and experience. What has been the cost?

3. Have you tended to look at the church primarily as an industry or as a garden? Discuss some of the implications of embracing an organic view of the church.

4. When things go wrong in the Kingdom, how do we discern whether it is punishment, discipline, testing, or simply an opportunity for greater faith in the Father?

5. What does Jesus mean by "seek first his kingdom" (Matthew 6:33)? And how do we let go of building our own kingdoms in order to better wait on (serve) His Kingdom?

POSTSCRIPT

The journey toward a still heart that waits on God and hears Him is a journey into new territory for many of us. In our activist culture, we minimize stillness and attentiveness. We always have something to do and something to produce. People always need us, and everything needs to have a practical or profitable purpose.

But waiting is more a state of heart than an activity. We might look for something like *Six Steps to Good Waiting,* but we usually want a simplified approach in order to control or guarantee the outcome. If the quick steps don't work, we want to return the book for a full refund, as though waiting should ever *work.*

Waiting is more a state of heart than an activity.

If someone pays attention to us simply to further his own cause, we consider it manipulative. If he is pleased that his waiting on us "worked," it's likely to irritate us. Waiting on others isn't about achieving an end of our own. Rather, it positions us to serve *their* ends.

Waiting on God means adopting a posture of attentiveness to

Him, while at the same time we grow aware of the possibilities that lie within the experience. And when the Lord speaks, He expects us to respond, much as He intended Noah to get on with the job He prescribed for him. Have we learned to respond to the Lord's leading or do we prefer our own agenda? It's a crucial question.

Perhaps as with Abraham, the Father wants to establish in us a new level of trust because we have started to hold a little too tightly to temporary things, things we now love just a little more than we love Him.

Maybe, like Moses, we wait on the Lord for a long season because He intends that we *un*learn some deep-seated and misguided values (independence, self-sufficiency, self-confidence). The season in the wilderness is a season for both self-awareness and God-awareness.

Or like David, we wait on God specifically as an expression of worship. Waiting on the Lord is not only about work, trust, or transformation, but worship. And we respond to it thus.

We may find that waiting on God during a period of suffering—like Jesus did—challenges us more than anything else. But we also discover that we learn new levels of obedience and experience His faithfulness in new ways.

Clearly, waiting on God is not a pointless exercise. Nor should we consider it a waste of time. In reality, it becomes the most profitable and transforming choice of our lives. And as we make it our lifestyle, it becomes a fountain of change flowing *through* us and *from* us to others.

A WORLD THAT WAITS FOR NOTHING

The greatest obstacle we face in "waiting on God" is our inexperience in waiting for anything.

In the classic 1971 film *Willy Wonka and the Chocolate Factory*, based on Roald Dahl's 1964 book, Willy Wonka offers a tour of his extraordinary factory to a few people lucky enough to find a golden ticket in their Wonka Chocolate Bar. "Wonka fever" strikes the country, and Veruca Salt, the precocious daughter of a magnate, complains bitterly and constantly about her father's staff's inability to find a golden ticket "the very first day." She refuses to go to school until a ticket is found, despite her father's pleading with her to give him time, saying that his staff has been working from dawn to dusk for three days straight tearing open boxes of the chocolate bars. Veruca bellows in response: "Make 'em work nights!" At last they find a golden ticket.

On the day of the tour, Veruca pushes ahead of other guests to be the first to enter the chocolate kingdom. Then throughout the early part of the tour, she grows increasingly aggressive, declaring, "I want it, and I want it now!" Eventually she is ejected from the chocolate factory, much to the relief of those who remain on the tour.[1]

In many ways, sadly, the obnoxious and demanding Veruca Salt is alive and well in our own day.

Fast food, the quick fix, "three easy steps," and "buy now, pay later"—instant gratification—seriously erode our ability to wait on God. Nevertheless, waiting and attentiveness take on a different shape over time, not as things we *do,* but as a way of life.

On the one hand, we pay a high price to live in such a way. Figuratively speaking, it means side streets, not freeways, between destinations. It means adopting countercultural values, minimizing the pursuit of personal ambition, and adopting a substantially different worldview.

On the other hand, we pay a high price *not* to live in such a way. If we choose to embrace the pace and the self-centeredness of the world around us, we choose to also embrace the futility, the frustration, and the ultimate failure of that same world.

If we aspire to wait more on the Lord, we must prepare ourselves for change and conflict. Sometimes that conflict will arise *within* us as we struggle with our own choices and priorities. At other times, that conflict will arise *between* us as we find ourselves pursuing different values than our peers.

Weight-loss coaches tell us that "fat friends have fat friends." As we hang out together and overeat together, we also put on the pounds together. And since we're all doing it together we feel a little less self-conscious and find it easier to excuse our increasing obesity. This subtle—perhaps sinister—reality contributes to our general poor health, but we ignore it because we're all unhealthy together.

Do we have the strength of will, courageous character, and yielded hearts to turn the tide, not in our eating habits (though we may need that, too), but in our waiting habits? And waiting *is* a habit.

DESIRE AND INTENTIONALITY

Sacred waiting—waiting on God—requires both desire and intentionality. We won't grow attentive to Him over the long haul unless we *want* to be attentive to Him. Perhaps this becomes our first prayer: "Father, increase my desire for you." He specializes in touching our hearts, and this prayer is a good start. Until we align our hearts with His, we'll struggle to wait on Him—to be attentive or to serve.

We often pray an equally short but quite different prayer: "Father, bless my work for you." But in that prayer we seek effectiveness, not intimacy; we request empowerment, not desire; we want success, not union with Him. Until we reach the point that we yearn for intimacy with the Father more than anything else—and as the springboard for everything else—we'll spin our wheels in service.

Thomas Kelly, an early twentieth-century Quaker with deep spiritual insights, called it the "God-intoxicated life."[2] By that he meant a life consumed with God himself. The focus of such a life is not on accomplishments we might present to Him but on the age-old quest to "know Him."

In 1996, Jan Johnson, a prolific author and speaker, wrote:

> I had complicated the spiritual life. . . . In truth, I needed only
> one thing—God. I didn't need a great quiet time, I needed a
> God-centered lifetime. I saw that my responsibility as a Christian
> was to seek God's company, not to seek spiritual maturity.[3]

Johnson does not intend to demean the value of the "quiet
time" or dismiss the responsibility and duty of the believer, but
she places them within the more vital context of intimacy with
God. So many of us see ourselves primarily as servants rather
than as sons of the living God. Like
the prodigal son in Luke 15, we keep
hoping that if we offer to work as a
hired hand, the Father will accept us.
We struggle to simply enjoy His Presence and His love.

*We have unnecessarily
complicated the
spiritual life.*

We have unnecessarily complicated
the spiritual life. And in many ways we
have made it burdensome. A. W. Tozer
cut through the foggy thinking when he wrote that the besetting
problem we face is that we live with a *God-and* philosophy.

> When religion has said its last word, there is little that we need
> other than God Himself. The evil habit of seeking *God-and*
> effectively prevents us from finding God in full revelation. In
> the *and* lies our great woe. If we omit the *and* we shall soon find
> God, and in Him we shall find that for which we have all our
> lives been secretly longing.[4]

Perhaps it's the *ands* that have prevented us from discovering intimacy with Christ and fully waiting on Him.

Throughout this book, we've seen some of the factors that

create an environment for meaningful sacred waiting. Like waiters and waitresses in a restaurant, Scripture calls us to wait *on* God rather than *for* God. This is our vocation, our life calling. And training to wait effectively at His table includes *work, trust, transformation, worship, obedience, service, submission, fasting, prayer, integrity, humility, patience, hope, and the Holy Spirit.* How much do these terms define or describe your life?

Waiting on God leads us to pursue greater intimacy with God. And the most basic elements of that waiting are presence and service. We've seen it in the lives of the saints. Will the Father see it in us? We've observed it in the stories underlying the church calendar. Will the Father observe it in our story?

The abundant life of which Jesus spoke (John 10:10) awaits all of us as we learn to wait on Him. May He bless us as we turn more to Him than to ourselves and serve His will rather than our own as waiters and waitresses in His Kingdom.

ENDNOTES

Introduction

1. Ben Woolsey and Matt Schulz, "Credit Card Statistics, Industry Facts, Debt Statistics 2006–2009," *www.creditcards.com/credit-card-news/credit-card-industry-facts-personal-debt-statistics-1276.php#ownership*.
2. Richard Wiseman, "Pace of Life: A Quirkology Experiment," *www.paceoflife.co.uk*.
3. For the full article—and much more detail—see Gene Weingarten, "Pearls Before Breakfast," *Washington Post* (April 8, 2007): *www.washingtonpost.com/wp-dyn/content/article/2007/04/04/AR2007040401721.html*.
4. Henri J. M. Nouwen, "Waiting for God," in *Watch for the Light: Readings for Advent and Christmas* (Maryknoll, NY: Orbis Books, 2004), 27.

Chapter 1

1. CBS News, "Starbucks Employees Take Espresso 101" (2/27/2008): *www.cbsnews.com/stories/2008/02/27/business/printable3882065.shtml*.
2. See "Methuselah," *www.christiananswers.net/dictionary/methuselah.html*. An alternative meaning might be "man of the javelin" (*www.newadvent.org/cathen/10048b.htm*), though none of these meanings carry absolute certainty.
3. The *Titanic* the world's largest passenger ship in its day, was launched in 1912. It measured 882' 9" long, 92' wide (beam), and 64' high (aft), *http://users.senet.com.au/~gittins/dimensions.html*. The deck area calculation and its adequacy for the ark can be found at Stanley Taylor and Paul Taylor, "Could Noah's Ark Really Hold All the Animals that Were Supposed to Be Preserved from the Flood?" *www.christiananswers.net/q-eden/edn-c013.html*.
4. The gopher tree (Genesis 6:14 KJV) remains unknown to our day; neither is it mentioned anywhere else in the Bible other than in the story of the flood.
5. Genesis 7:6–13 indicates that Noah and his family entered the ark on the seventeenth day of the second month of his six hundredth year. Genesis 8:13–16 indicates that Noah and his family finally left the ark when the earth was dry, on the twenty-seventh day of the second month of his six hundredth and first year.
6. Barbara Brown Taylor, *Leaving Church: A Memoir of Faith* (New York: Harper-Collins, 2006), 134.

Chapter 2

1. See *www.britannica.com/EBchecked/topic/255841/Haran* for more background and historical information on Haran.
2. See Genesis 12:7; 13:14–17; 15:5.
3. Barbara Brown Taylor, *When God Is Silent* (Cambridge, MA: Cowley Publications, 1998), 63.
4. U.S. Department of Justice, Office of Justice Programs, "Gun Violence in the United States," *http://ojjdp.ncjrs.org/pubs/gun_violence/sect01.html*.
5. William Law, *A Serious Call to a Devout and Holy Life* (New York: Vintage Books, 2002), 56.

Chapter 3

1. Michael Dorman, "The Killing of Kitty Genovese, " *www.newsday.com/community/guide/lihistory/ny-history-hs818a,0,7944135.story.*

2. Horeb and Mount Sinai are synonymous. On this mountain Moses not only saw the burning bush but later received the Ten Commandments from the Lord. Most contemporary scholars believe that Jebel Musa, which rises 2,244 meters above sea level, is probably the ancient Horeb. St. Catherine's Monastery has stood at the foot of that mountain since the middle of the sixth century.

3. Alfred Delp, *Advent of the Heart* (San Francisco: Ignatius Press, 2006), 149.

4. Brennan Manning, *Abba's Child* (Colorado Springs: NavPress, 2002), 28.

5. Henri J.M. Nouwen, *The Wounded Healer* (Garden City, NY: Image Books, 1979), 92–94.

Chapter 4

1. Eugene H. Peterson, *Working the Angles: The Shape of Pastoral Integrity* (Grand Rapids, MI: Eerdmans, 1987), 41.

2. Nicolaus Copernicus (1473–1543) published his seminal work—*On the Revolutions of the Celestial Spheres*—at the very end of his life. His book postulated a sun-centered view of the universe.

3. Second Samuel 1:18 refers to "the Book of Jashar" (literally "the upright one"), which possibly also contained songs David had contributed. This book likely contained national songs and poems that extolled the heroic deeds of Israel's leaders, but it has long since been lost. See also Joshua 10:13.

4. Charles Haddon Spurgeon, *The Treasury of David* (Nashville: Thomas Nelson, 1984), Vol. 1, 46.

5. Psalm 25 is the first acrostic psalm that we have, with each of the twenty-two verses commencing with a new letter of the Hebrew alphabet in their proper order.

6. Thomas Merton, *No Man Is an Island* (Boston: Shambhala, 2005), 16.

Chapter 5

1. Owen Crouch, *Expository Preaching and Teaching—Hebrews* (Joplin, MO: College Press Publishing, 1983), 146.

2. Dave Cullen, "Who Said 'Yes'?" Salon.com News (9/30/1999): *www.salon.com/news/feature/1999/09/30/bernall.* Immediately after the Columbine school massacre, stories circulated that Cassie Bernall, another student, had been confronted about her faith and died as a martyr, refusing to deny Christ. Despite the subsequent bestselling book by her mother, Misty Bernall (*She Said Yes: The Unlikely Martyrdom of Cassie Bernall*), eye-witness accounts of the incident generally now refute the exchange with Bernall and attribute the mix-up to the more verified exchange with Valeen Schnurr.

3. William Barclay, *The Letter to the Hebrews,* revised ed., Daily Bible Study Series (Philadelphia: Westminster Press, 1976), 47.

4. Ibid., 48.

5. Richard Felix, *The School of Dying Graces* (Carol Stream, IL: Salt River Books, Tyndale House Publishers, 2004), 8.

6. Sheldon Vanauken, *A Severe Mercy* (New York: HarperOne, 1987).

7. Richard Rohr, "Utterly Humbled by Mystery" (December 18, 2006): *www. npr.org/templates/story/story.php?storyId=6631954.*

8. Larry Crabb, *The Pressure's Off: There's a New Way to Live* (Colorado Springs: Waterbrook Press, 2004), 18.

9. This title for Christ, *The Lamb,* occurs frequently throughout Revelation— twenty-nine times. The title evokes the specific image of the sacrificial or Passover lamb. Thus in the Revelation it is identified explicitly with slaughter and blood. Jesus is the "Lamb that was slain," in 5:12; 13:8. In 5:6, He is the Lamb who looks as if He has been slain. And in 7:14–15; 12:11, we have a reference to "the blood of the Lamb." This allusion to the Lamb–explicitly linked with the sacrificial motif—is intended to evoke faith in the Mutual Sufferer.

Chapter 6

1. Find a useful analysis of some of the social themes undergirding *A Christmas Carol* at "A Christmas Carol," Wikipedia, *http://en.wikipedia.org/wiki/A_Christmas_Carol.*

2. Alfred Delp, *Advent of the Heart* (San Francisco: Ignatius Press, 2006), 53.

3. Ibid.

Chapter 7

1. For a brief analysis of Lent, see Ted Olsen, "The Beginning of Lent," *Christianity Today* (August 8, 2008): *www.christianitytoday.com/ch/news/2004/lent.html.* For more detailed information about the structure of Lent and additional links, see Kenneth Collins, "The Season of Lent," *www.kencollins.com/holy-04.htm.*

2. *The Sayings of the Desert Fathers,* Benedicta Ward, trans. (Kalamazoo, MI: Cistercian Publications, 1984), Arsenius, 1, 9.

3. Henri J.M. Nouwen, *The Way of the Heart: Desert Spirituality and Contemporary Ministry* (San Francisco: HarperSanFrancisco, 1981), 15.

4. Ibid., 31–32.

5. Sterling Hundley, "Not a Fast Fix," *Christianity Today* (April 5, 1999): 31.

6. Frederica Mathewes-Green, "To Hell on a Cream Puff," *Christianity Today* (November 13, 1995): *www.christianitytoday.com/ct/2000/augustweb-only/23.0c.html?start=1.*

Chapter 8

1. A more extensive summary of the rescue effort can be found at Jeremy Zakis, "Australian Landslide: Rescue at Thredbo Ski Resort," *9-1-1 Magazine* (Mar./ Apr. 1998): *www.9-1-1magazine.com/magazine/1998/0398/features/52zakis.html* and "1997 Thredbo Landslide," Wikipedia, *http://en.wikipedia.org/wiki/1997_Thredbo_landslide.* Stuart Diver later coauthored (with Simon Bouda) his own account of the harrowing ordeal in *Survival: The Inspirational Story of the Thredbo Disaster's Sole Survivor* (Sydney, Australia: Pan Macmillan, 1999).

2. Matt Peckham, blogging for *PC World,* noted that the worldwide interactive entertainment industry was on track to achieve revenues of $57 billion by 2009. *http://blogs.pcworld.com/gameon/archives/007189.html.*

3. Thomas à Kempis, *The Imitation of Christ* (Notre Dame, IN: Ave Maria Press, 2001), Book 2, chapter 11, 77.

4. P. T. Forsyth, *The Soul of Prayer* (Vancouver: Regent College Publishing, 2002), 47.

5. Thomas Merton, *No Man Is an Island* (Boston: Shambhala, 2005), 86.

Chapter 9

1. By the early New Testament period, Shavuot had lost most of its association with agriculture and instead focused almost exclusively on God's gracious gift of the Torah (the Law) on Mount Sinai. Modern Judaism continues to celebrate the giving of the Torah rather than agriculture. For much more detail, see *www.chabad.org/holidays/shavuot/default_cdo/jewish/Shavuot.htm*.

2. See John 21 for the full account. Verse 2 names Simon Peter—it's interesting that his old name *Simon* is reattached—Thomas, Nathanael, the sons of Zebedee—James, John—"and two other disciples."

3. In the original Greek text, we find a significant contrast of words. The first two times, Jesus asks Peter if he loves Him, and uses the strong term *agape* (which I have translated "love" here). Each time Peter replies, he uses the weaker term *phileo* (which I have translated "think fondly of"). On the third question (v. 17), Jesus changes His language and uses the weaker term *phileo*, to which Peter replies a third time with the term *phileo*. Peter clearly resists claiming to have agape love for Christ at that time and admits to only phileo love.

4. Some of this material first appeared in an article I published in 2008. David Timms, "No More Inventories, Please," *The LOOKOUT* (December 14, 2008): 8–10, *www.lookoutmag.com/articles/articledisplay.asp?id=591*.

5. I base this simple definition on Ephesians 4:11–13, which suggests that gifts were given, ultimately, that we might all "become mature, attaining to the whole measure of the fullness of Christ" (v. 13).

Chapter 10

1. Joni Eareckson Tada, "Christian Quotes," *www.dailychristianquote.com/dcqtada.html*.

2. David Fisher, "Pilgrim Scribblings," *http://pilgrimscribblings.blogspot.com/2007/05/god-sells-some-cows.html*. The story also appears in print in Steven Lawson, *Absolutely Sure* (Sisters, OR: Multnomah, 2006).

3. See Genesis 1:26–28. This Dominion Principle affirms that we are made in the image of God to reign. It has significant implications on this topic of our kingdom and the Kingdom of God, which I unpack in more detail in *Living the Lord's Prayer* (Minneapolis: Bethany House, 2008), 99–113.

Postscript

1. Julie Dawn Cole portrayed the petulant and impatient Veruca Salt in the film. She sang and recorded the song "I Want It Now" on her thirteenth birthday. Ironically, Veruca's trashing of the Golden Egg Room required a total of thirty-six takes. "Veruca Salt," Wikipedia, *http://en.wikipedia.org/wiki/Veruca_Salt*.

2. Thomas Kelly, *A Testament of Devotion* (San Francisco: HarperSanFrancisco, 1992), 32.

3. Jan Johnson, *Enjoying the Presence of God: Discovering Intimacy with God in the Daily Rhythms of Life* (Colorado Springs: NavPress, 1996), 11.

4. A. W. Tozer, *The Pursuit of God* (Camp Hill, PA: Christian Publications, 1993), 18.